Genpo Roshi's groundbreaking book offers us tools sprung up from the merging of Eastern work. It helps us to see and know ourselves with clarity, to be less attached to limited egocentric perspectives, and to function freely as integrated human beings — effectively bringing anyone who applies these methods the experience of a free, fulfilling, and joyous awakened life. I myself have found it both useful and illumining.

> — *Lama Surya Das, author of Awakening the Buddha Within: Tibetan Wisdom for the Western World*

To shift perspectives easily, to see the world from another's point of view, is an essential skill that is taught by this book. It has the potential to enhance every aspect of our lives.

> — *Michael Zimmerman, Attorney, Mediator, Zen Teacher Former Chief Justice of the Utah Supreme Court*

In these times of such great global need, Genpo Merzel brings a method that will not tell leaders what to do, but rather, will help them know themselves from the widest possible perspective. May it benefit them, and us all.

> —*Glenna M. Crooks, PhD, Pres. & CEO, Strategic Health Policy International.*

Genpo Roshi's book brings us into the immediacy of his face to face teaching, inviting us to listen to, rather than argue with, the voices in our heads whose incessant chatter creates the illusion of self. Freed from the need to silence or censor, Big Mind teaches us how to slip the knots of small mind and take refuge in the One Mind that is all minds and none.

> — *Rabbi Rami Shapiro, author of Sacred Art of Loving Kindness*

Big Mind is nothing short of a springboard to an evolutionary leap forward in consciousness, deftly transforming an already proven and powerful clinical technique into a nearly effortless process for discovering the purest, most transcendent experience of Who We Truly Are. He compassionately strikes at the very heart of what ails us in these troubled times, giving followers of all religious traditions an amazingly simple and effective way to transcend their differences and reach previously unattainable levels of spiritual development and insight — all while still honoring and supporting every tradition's unique approach to the Divine. Honestly, the potential Big Mind holds for our future is just staggering.

> — *Major Stuart Lloyd, USAF, Asst. Professor of Behavioral Sciences & Leadership, United States Air Force Academy*

In my personal life, in my professional life as an attorney, and in my spiritual life as a Mormon Bishop, the Big Mind process has proven to be both foundational and transformational. Genpo Roshi has discovered a way to make available to everyone without being in conflict with virtually anyone's deeply held beliefs, an immediate glimpse of Big Mind, Big Heart and other transcendent states as well as practices which will profoundly deepen one's capacity to stabilize and integrate experience of the Absolute with enlightened functioning in the world. I can recommend this book without reservation as a wonderful introduction to this astonishing teaching.

— *John T. Kesler, Bishop of the LDS Church, Attorney*

As a Rabbi I share with all mankind a quest not only for spiritual truth but a longing for greater knowledge of my inner essence, my true identity and my mission on earth. How remarkable that Genpo Roshi, a Buddhist, captures so many of the insights that help me pursue my own journey for ultimate — and universal truth. I experienced first hand the fruits of this incredible method and I'm delighted to see it now in print in a format that will certainly help many thousands gain a deeper understanding of their link with the One and the One-ness of all of Creation.

— *Rabbi Benjamin Blech, author of Understanding Judaism*

A brilliant breakthrough in spiritual practice. It helps people 'get' what ordinarily would take years, even decades of sitting meditation. Genpo's acknowledgement of his personal vulnerability and his own struggles is particularly helpful, as is his lack of judgement of the aspects of our selves that many people feel shame about or aversion towards. I've always thought that approaches that emphasized attaining non-dual states left many people unintegrated and unable to function well in the world. The section on embracing and going beyond dual and non-dual is a stroke of genius.

— *Bill Harris, Director, Centrepointe Research Institute*

This brilliant book presents a marriage of traditional Zen practice and Western therapeutic technique allowing readers to step out of their egos and make a complete shift in their normal perspective. The simple and effective yet profound Big Mind process gives readers the opportunity to awaken to the experience of their own True Nature, Ground of Being or Ultimate Reality. It is open to people of all spiritual traditions and paths. Anyone can do this. I highly recommend this book to all who wish to integrate their regular everyday selves with their unborn, undying, infinite nature and in so doing to realise that they have never been apart. As an added bonus the reader is given an intimate account of the spiritual path, development and maturing insight of a traditional Zen master.

— *David Scott, PhD, Pres., Uechi-Ryu Karate Association, UK, 6th Dan*
author of The Elements of Zen

This book is the missing manual for the human mind. Every human should receive it at birth.

— *Ottmar Liebert, Composer and Guitarist*

As a physician I see fear, isolation and mind/body/spirit disconnect contributing to illness today. I see the antidote as Big Mind/Big Heart, Genpo Roshi, and this book as a revolutionary innovation which holds the key to integrated wellness.

— *Kamilla Buddemeier MD, F.A.C.C.*

I would not ordinarily choose this kind of a book to read but I am truly glad I did. It is a good reminder of what we intuitively know, and a good reminder to practice that which we intuitively know. It brings to light the internal dilemmas we experience when confronted with ideas different from those we are used to experiencing. Big Mind/Big Heart will help us learn and practice the tolerance and mutual understanding we all need in our ever-shrinking world.

— *Carol Merzel Jacobs*

Big Mind/Big Heart is truly a gift, accessible to anyone interested in awakening to a more conscious, fulfilled life. Genpo Roshi masterfully guides us through a deeply healing process that integrates Zen wisdom with the insight of Western psychology. This simple, profound approach takes us beyond our limited selves to realize our inherent wholeness, so that we may bring our world more of the clarity, compassion and joy that it so desperately needs.

— *Paul D. Thielking, MD, Psychiatrist*

This is a book full of heart. It blends the groundbreaking Voice Dialogue method developed by Hal and Sidra Stone with the deep Eastern understanding of the awakened states, and the author's own beautifully digested and integrated realization. He opens the essence of Zen understanding to the reader, holding nothing back. More than that, he provides a tool, the Big Mind process, so that this same understanding can be glimpsed by a beginner and refined by a long-term practitioner. I have witnessed the stunning effect of the process regardless of a person's age, circumstances, and spiritual background. Not only does one learn a great deal from this book, one also receives the gift of no fear by taking it to heart and making the Big Mind process a natural part of one's everyday practice.

— *Zen Master Nicolee Jikyo McMahon, Psychotherapist*

Today's business and political crises demand innovative approaches and new perspectives. Even for those completely uninterested in seeking religious solutions, this book presents a critical key: a panorama of the self so varied, and ultimately so expansive, that the capability to shift perspectives becomes a natural discipline. Whether the functioning of your life requires better thinking, creating, negotiating or problem-solving, this book will set you on a path to much readier access of a Big Mind.

— *Pat Trifunov, VP, GlaxoSmithKline*

It seems we spend decades pursuing our gifts and strengths, or wallowing in our problems, in an attempt to find personal clarity. But no matter all that effort, life still remains utterly confusing. With Genpo Merzel though, I learned more from him in that first hour than I did 15 years as an athlete. For starters, I realized I didn't have to risk my life to feel brilliant — it can happen just sitting in a chair, experientially. What a relief.

— *Kristen Ulmer, Extreme Skier*
Voted best overall female skier in the world 12 years in a row

This book is an extraordinary contribution to the integration of personal and spiritual growth, combining powerful psychological insights with timeless wisdom teachings.

—*Frances Vaughan, PhD, Psychologist, author of Shadows of the Sacred*

Genpo Roshi has developed a path to insight for the many who have neither the time nor the disposition for long Zen training. This is a work of compassionate outreach for people of all faiths, or no faith at all.

— *Zen Master, Father Robert Jinsen Kennedy, S.J.*
author of Zen Gifts to Christians

Big Mind · Big Heart

Finding Your Way

ALSO BY DENNIS GENPO MERZEL

*The Path of the Human Being: Zen Teachings on
the Bodhisattva Way*

24/7 Dharma: Impermanence, No-Self, Nirvana

Beyond Sanity and Madness: The Way of Zen Master Dogen

The Eye Never Sleeps: Striking to the Heart of Zen

Big Mind/Big Heart Revealed (DVD)

The Path of the Human Being (DVD)

*The author's talks using the Big Mind process with a live
audience can be viewed at www.zeneye.org*

Big Mind · Big Heart
Finding Your Way

Dennis Genpo Merzel

PUBLISHING

SALT LAKE CITY

Cover photo and photo on page 191 by Dave Labrum, with Busath Photography, Salt Lake City, Utah. Used with permission

CD Recording of Big Mind session with Dennis Genpo Merzel and Sheila Hamilton recorded Feb. 2004. Used with permission.

CD Recording of Guided Meditation session with Dennis Genpo Merzel produced by Bruce Lambson.

Big Mind™ is a registered trademark of Big Mind, Inc.

For information contact:

BIG MIND PUBLISHING
1268 EAST SOUTH TEMPLE
SALT LAKE CITY, UTAH 84102
www.bigmind.org

Library of Congress Cataloging in Publication Data

Merzel, Dennis Genpo, 1944-
 Big mind, big heart : finding your way / Dennis Genpo Merzel.
   p. cm.
 ISBN 978-0-9771423-3-0 (pbk.)
 1.   Spiritual life — Zen Buddhism. I. Title

 BQ9288.M48 2007
 294.3'44 4— dc22
                              2007012004

Printed in the United States of America   10 9 8 7 6 5 4 3

Dedication

Because this book is the fruit of all the teaching, coaching, mentoring, and unconditional love that I have received during my lifetime from these people, I dedicate it to:

Coaches in Earlier Years:
Dick Hammer · Tom Parks · Frank A. Kanarek · Jack Watkins
Jerry LaBonte · Monte Nitzkowski · Bob Horn
Jim Schultz · Whitey Saari

Mentors:
Annette Gromfin · Everett Shostrum · Hal & Sidra Stone

Teachers:
Taizan Maezumi Roshi
Bernie Tetsugen Glassman Roshi · Koun Yamada Roshi
Chögyam Trungpa Rinpoche · Seung Sahn Sunim

Family:
Ben & Lillian Merzel · Willard & Gene Young
My wife, Stephanie Young Merzel
Carol Merzel Jacobs · Tai Bennett Merzel · Nicole Li Merzel
Tiby the Temple Dog Merzel · Fillette Little Sister Merzel

Acknowledgements

I want to offer my thanks to Ken Wilber for encouraging me to write this book and for his most enthusiastic Foreword. Also to Hal and Sidra Stone for the inspiration and encouragement they have given me in my work, and for their generous introductory remarks to this book.

I also want to give thanks to those people who read the manuscript at various stages and took the trouble to give me their suggestions on it, and to those who offered advance comments, some of which appear on the cover and early pages of this volume.

I owe a deep debt of gratitude to Mark and Margaret Esterman for all their great work in transcribing and editing this book. I wrote it in ten days while on a trip to Hawaii with my children, typing on my Blackberry and dictating portions of it by phone. They have now worked for ten months to make it readable and presentable. Without their help the book would have taken much longer and would not have been such a pleasure to write. We've had a great time.

Contents

Foreword

Ken Wilber

Let me state this as strongly as I can: **the Big Mind process founded by Zen Master Dennis Genpo Merzel is arguably the most important and original discovery in the last two centuries of Buddhism.** It is an astonishingly original, profound, and effective path for waking up, or seeing one's True Nature. It is such a simple and universal practice it can be used in any spiritual path you wish, or even by itself, as a practice for realizing your True Self, which you can call God, Allah, Jahweh, Brahman, Tao, Ein Sof; it doesn't really matter, because the core of the Big Mind process is Emptiness itself, which, having no specific content at all, can and does embrace anything that arises, integrating it all.

In Zen, this realization of one's True Nature, or Ultimate Reality, is called *kensho* or *satori* ("seeing into one's True Nature," or discovering Big Mind and Big Heart). It often takes many years of extremely difficult practice (I know, I've done it) in order for a profound satori to occur. With the Big Mind process, as in Zen, a kensho or glimpse of your True Nature can occur suddenly — I have witnessed it repeatedly. Once you get it, you can do it virtually any time you wish, and almost instantaneously. It is nothing less than the discovery of your True and Unique Self, Ultimate Reality, the Ground of All Being — again, call it what you like, for "they call it Many which is really One." Of course, this initial — but very strong—insight or kensho can be infinitely deepened with continuous practice, and Genpo gives simple instructions for how to continue meditating to deepen this awakening. But awaken you will, I truly believe.

Genpo didn't derive this process exclusively from Buddhism. He took some of the central discoveries of Western psychology — particularly Voice Dialogue and subpersonalities — and found an astonishingly effective way to integrate the best of the East (or simply the best of the contemplative traditions) — with some of the best of the West (namely, working not with Infinite Reality but with finite reality and with finite selves, helping to make them conscious and then healed and whole). The wondrous part is that he then found an easy and effective way to integrate the Infinite and the finite selves.

The Big Mind process works with your own mind, with your states of consciousness, just as they are now. What you may not know, if you haven't had a satori or awakening of some sort, is that right now, reading this page, is Big Mind, or God, or Spirit. And it is so close and so obvious that you can't see it. But this book (which is a simple handbook of how to do Big Mind/Big Heart practice yourself), will show you that part of your own awareness, which is **already enlightened**, already one with Spirit, already fully awakened. Once you spot that, an entirely different world opens for you. The book you have in your hands right now will, I can almost guarantee it, open your mind's eye and show you how, in this very instant, your True Self is fully and completely present, looking through your eyes, listening with your ears, holding this book in its hands: right now! And it always has been, but it was too close to see, too obvious to notice, too simple to believe. This extraordinary discovery awaits you in this book.

We at Integral Institute have found this process to be so effective and profound, that we have made it a central part of our programs, seminars, and Integral Life Practice. We have found the process to be close to 100% effective, and that is why I feel comfortable promising, or darn close to promising, that by the time you finish reading this book, you will be among the enlightened ones, even if with beginner's eyes.

Genpo did not include developmental psychology in this integration of the best of East and West, and for a reason: it simply does not matter what stage of development you are at in order to do the Big Mind process. It works at virtually any major stage of development — whether you are at magic, mythic, rational, pluralistic, integral, or super-integral: any stage can do Big Mind and awaken to the ever-present, all-pervading, infinite Reality of All Being (again, name it as you wish). If you want, you can study how these stages mesh with the states of Big Mind: Genpo Roshi is a founding member of Integral Spiritual Center at Integral Institute, and has been instrumental in studying ways to fit together stages of consciousness with states of consciousness, as I have explained in my own book, Integral Spirituality.

But start here, with this book, and this simple, profound process, and be prepared to find your own True Self, possibly for the first time, but joyous in any event. Here you will learn to **integrate** the **finite or dualistic selves** (the Skeptic, the Controller, the Victim, the Damaged Self, Anger, the Seeking Mind, etc.) with the **Infinite or Non-dual Self** in its many displays (Big Mind, Big Heart, Integrated Feminine/Masculine Compassion, Great Joy, Great Gratitude, Integrated Free-Functioning Human Being). A genuine taste of all of this awaits your reading pleasure, my friend, and I am happy and hopeful for you that you will simply relax the mind, rest in the present, let your consciousness go free, for it has no walls — and then read this book, or simply let it soak into you, let the words wash through you, and soon enough, that "you" will be "YOU" — which is to say, I AMness, your own True, Infinite, and Eternal Nature. This book is truly a handbook of Awakening to I AMness, which is already looking out of your eyes right now.

I am adding my own blessings to this book's wonderful words of awakening, and may the merit of all of this be dedicated to sentient beings everywhere, that they too may wake up and discover who, and what, they really are. In Big Mind suffering can find no purchase, hatred and anger can find no home. In Big Heart gratitude and joy inexplicably arise in their place, dancing wildly in the deepest clarity and most astonishing thankfulness. Big Mind/Big Heart provide an endless fountain of awakened joy, happiness, compassion, and wisdom, pouring out of your mind and your heart and into the world in a gushing and uncontrollably overflowing superabundance of radiance, release, bliss, luminosity, celebration, and joy.

Now look at me, my friend, and listen, please, I'm truly serious: isn't it time for you to wake up? How long have you been lost in this dream? Can't you feel the wisdom holders shaking you, saying, "Wake up, please, this is just a dream!" You know this, don't you? You know that in the deepest part of your being, you can wake up, don't you? You have been searching for how long now? Well, it is time for the Great Search to end. As long as you are searching, you are looking for a future moment that will be better than this moment, but it is this moment that holds the entire key: why are you running away from your own awakening?

So stop searching, take a breath, and start reading this manual for Awakening to the present moment, and I think you will never be able to look back. And then, if you and I ever meet, we will know each other, won't we? With a twinkle in your eye, a slight smile on your face, a radiance in your heart, you and I will look into the eyes of each other and see the one and only Self, Big Mind, Big

Heart, and the days and nights of the endless search will have lost its dreadfully painful meaning.

And we will have Dennis Genpo Merzel Roshi to thank, for discovering a simple and original process of Awakening right now. And so I offer the deepest bow to Genpo, offer the merit to all sentient beings, and into your hands, with infinite blessings, I now pass on this extraordinary book to you.

Denver, Colorado
February 2007

Introduction

Hal Stone, Ph.D. & Sidra Stone, Ph.D.

This book is about the journey of a remarkable man. Genpo Roshi was Western born and raised, but his own spiritual nature, which emerged early in life, was not to be ignored. Zen Buddhism has been the vessel that carried this teacher's profound spiritual experiences.

We first met Genpo Roshi in 1983 when he was the senior teacher at the Zen Center in Los Angeles. Hal's immediate reaction to him was extremely positive. The situation at the center was very challenging and here was a man who was behaving with the highest degree of thoughtfulness and practical wisdom. It was at this time that Hal brought a staff to the Zen Center and conducted a training for the Zen community in Voice Dialogue, Relationship and the Psychology of Selves. Later we provided ongoing groups to continue the training for those in the community who were interested.

A long period of time has passed since those years and we have watched the development of Genpo's work and his spiritual teachings with real pleasure. Most recently he has been focused on methods for activating the Big Mind. We are honored at his inclusion of some of the basic ideas of the Psychology of Selves and some aspects of the Voice Dialogue method in the development of his own original methodology for accessing the Big Mind energy.

Over the years, part of the pleasure of our own work is to see the creative ways with which people use both the Voice Dialogue method and the Psychology of Selves. There are many coaches and management consultants who have developed new language and new formats for working with business executives based on our work. Dance therapists and body-oriented therapists use it in their way to help people experience and clarify the many selves that make up the psyche and can be accessed through the body. Our work and our ideas have been used by spiritual seekers, astrologers, physicians, and scientists as well as by psychotherapists and counselors of many traditions. Many of these spiritual seekers who resonate with our work seem also to be drawn to Buddhism as a framework for their own search, seeing our work as an embodiment of basic Buddhist principles.

It is important to separate out the theory and application of the Psychology of Selves from the actual method of Voice Dialogue. The actual method of Voice Dialogue is a one on one procedure in which a trained facilitator is able to help a client to hold — and to explore — the energy of the client's different selves. The facilitator in this situation has no attachment to getting to any particular self or to accomplish anything specific with the self that is being addressed. For us, the goal of the work with selves is the development of an Aware Ego process that can hold opposites; the opposite energies or selves.

For some, however, the highest value is to be able to access certain selves that are valuable to people for specific reasons. For example, there are many facilitators who emphasize facilitating "being" energy because, as a result of our emphasis upon "doing" and achievement, it is lacking in the majority of people raised in our Western culture. This "being" energy often provides a first introduction to spiritual energy.

Another clear example of this emphasis upon a specific energy or self is the remarkable work of Judith Stone. Judith is one of the senior teachers of the Voice Dialogue work and she has developed a body of work that she calls Body Dialogue. In this approach, she is able to facilitate the body and many of its systems with the most amazing results. She uses Voice Dialogue for the specific purpose of teaching people how to tune in to their own bodies.

So it is that Genpo has used his knowledge of the Psychology of Selves and has developed his own unique application of the Voice Dialogue method. Rather than moving with the energies as they emerge, he specifically focuses on helping people experience the Big Mind and the many related spiritual selves. We live in a day and age when more and more people are thirsting for spiritual experience and Genpo provides this for an ever-increasing number of people.

Genpo is an explorer of the spiritual world and a powerful teacher. This book is a record of his explorations. In it, he teaches by using the dialogue approach with himself as the person whose selves are being facilitated. In this way, he allows many of the different spiritual voices within him to speak directly to the reader. This book is aimed at the spiritual seeker whose spiritual selves are similarly waiting to be "invited" to come forward and speak. The popularity of Genpo's work clearly indicates that there are many people whose selves come alive when invited out in this way, and that, for them, this work strikes a deeply resonant chord.

Albion, California
February, 2007

Preface

All of us are facing very challenging times. We are concerned for our children, parents, partners, friends and loved ones. We would like to be able to communicate and empathize more fully in all of our relationships. We want our children and family — and ourselves — to reach our fullest potential, to be happier and more joyful in this life.

Each day brings stress at work, worries about financial security, not to mention the threat of terrorism, dirty bombs, global warming and natural disasters. We are all searching for how to be more at peace with ourselves, to live with less fear, anger, and anxiety, simply to get through the day.

This book can help each of us work with these issues and problems. It offers what may be one of the best tools that has come from the merging of East and West. It will help you to work with your thoughts, feelings, and emotions, to gain a new perspective on your difficulties, to see how our basic attachment to the self and its notions keeps us suffering and feeling insecure. This book will help you to see yourself with clarity, to be less attached to a limited self-perspective, and therefore to function freely as an integrated human being.

It is the result of more than thirty-five years of study, difficulty, and searching for a way to bring anyone the experience of living a free, fulfilling and awakened life. I have written in a style that you don't have to be a Buddhist practitioner or scholar to comprehend. The point of the book is to make these highly valuable, accessible and urgently needed teachings available to the world.

My own path has led me to the Way of Zen, but there are many paths I could have taken which could have led me in the same direction. In fact, since I first developed the Big Mind process described in this book, I have shared it with thousands of people of all ages, from children and teenagers to the elderly and the terminally ill. It has worked for people in many walks of life — educators, doctors, therapists, CEO's and leaders in business and government, lawyers, judges and mediators, athletes and artists, among others — and of many different faiths — Catholic Priests and Nuns, Protestant Ministers, Mormon Bishops, Jewish Rabbis, Hindu Swamis, Buddhist Lamas and Zen Masters, skeptics and those of no particular religion. It has proven to be compatible with all faiths and beliefs, so I am confident all people can find it useful and valuable on the Way we all share.

1

Big Mind · Big Heart

Author's Note:

Readers who are not so familiar with either Zen or the Big Mind process might want to listen to the brief 15 minute example of the process on the CD accompanying the book (Track 1) even before getting into reading the book. This is part of a completely unrehearsed and spontaneous conversation with Sheila Hamilton, a young woman whom I had not met before, and who had no prior experience with Zen or Big Mind. I think you will enjoy it, and it will help you better understand the book.

T HERE is a transcendent awareness, a Big Mind, a Big Heart, present and readily accessible to each and every one of us. When we realize it, we see it is the source of true peace, happiness, satisfaction, courage and joy. And yet, we don't know how to access it, we don't know how to bring it into our awareness. We don't know how to manifest it or embody it.

For the past thirty-six years, I have been searching for a way to assist people to access this awareness. In June 1999, after much study and difficulty, I finally found a simple, effective way which I have been exploring and refining since then. I call it the Big Mind/ Big Heart process, or, simply, Big Mind.

In a way it all began over a weekend in early February of 1971 while I was camping with two friends in the Mojave Desert. Sitting alone at the top of a small mountain I was contemplating how at the age of twenty-six I could have already screwed up my life so badly. I was feeling trapped in a relationship that certainly hadn't started out that way. Earlier I had been in another relationship that left me feeling I needed to break out or I was going to go insane. Now less than three years later the same feelings were surfacing again. I had come out to the desert to get some space.

From the mountaintop I could see my VW camper parked a couple of miles away where we were planning to sleep the next two nights. I started thinking about my apartment back in Long Beach California, where I was teaching elementary school to Special Education children at the 4th, 5th, and 6th grade level, and where I lived across the street from the beach with my girlfriend. Two questions naturally arose in my mind: How could I be so screwed up, and where is home?

Where is home? That's a good beginning for all of us. In fact that is the beginning, when we first realize that there's something missing, something lacking. We don't know what it is. It's a mystery. Yet we have this sense, there's a kind of awakening to what we could call spirituality, or just awareness, and we begin to seek for what it is that is missing, because we don't have a clue what it is.

The awakened mind is always sending out a kind of signal. The awakened mind, whatever we want to call it, is always trying to emerge, always trying to call us home. Someone once said that our only ailment is homesickness, and that we're sick because we're not at home; and yet, of course, wherever we are is home. But we don't feel that; we feel alienated from our own home and from ourself.

So I think one of the things we're always looking for is how to be at home wherever we are, how to be home in our own body, how to be home in our self. It's like a homing instinct. We're like the pigeon that seems to have this amazing ability to find its way home.

I call it the Mind that Seeks the Way or the Truth. Sometimes that mind is not awakened. The moment it does awaken, our life really changes. At that moment our priorities seem to shift. A lot of the things that up until then seemed so important —security, fame, possessions, wealth — all those things suddenly seem to take a back seat. What becomes much more important is our own discovery of who we are.

That's what happened to me on that mountaintop in the middle of the Mojave Desert in 1971. All of a sudden everything dropped away and I experienced something totally new and completely unexpected. I became the Universe, one with the Creator and all Creations. I realized that all things are connected and interconnected, that everything is related to everything else and each thing in this world affects everything else in this world.

It was like going sane after being insane all my life. Of course my mother later interpreted this precisely the other way around. I felt for the first time that life made complete sense, and all my seeking for security, wealth, and fame were empty and ridiculous, and I was at peace. The only two things that really mattered now were sharing this experience with others and continuing to discover more about this amazing journey called life. These two desires have never ceased to inspire me. They are the motivation to write this story and this book.

I had no explanation at that time for what had just happened to me, but I knew intuitively it was huge. I would never be the same person who had climbed up to the top of that mountain. A powerful and indescribable energy was running through me. It was as if God and I were one. The entire world was me and I was the entire world. I am all things and all things are me. I felt as if all my life I had been going forward like a locomotive at a hundred miles an hour and suddenly I had made an abrupt U-turn and was going in precisely the opposite direction. Great compassion arose naturally without any effort. The only thing that mattered was waking up and helping others do the same.

Later that evening my friend said I seemed to be talking like a Zen Master. I didn't know the first thing about Zen Masters or Zen, but I couldn't sleep that entire night because the energy just kept flowing through me, as though I was a conduit for something greater than this limited body. In the morning I sat up in the camper realizing that my life was never going to be the same, and clear about what needed to be done. When I got back to Long Beach Sunday evening I broke up with my partner and began the journey that I am still on.

I think we all have a sense that there's something more, something greater. As kids we play with the mysterious concepts of infinity and eternity — I know I did. Sometimes it takes the form of wondering about God, or even death. Since I was raised with no particular religious faith, I had no particular beliefs about an afterlife. So I would think about when I die, what's that like, never ever being conscious again, for all eternity? That's kind of a scary thought.

There's a part of us that's always questioning and seeking. I remember talking to my sister Carol back in 1973, I was staying in her house in Marin County, and I said "Don't you ever ask these questions, who am I, and where am I going, and what is this all about, and why am I here?" She said, "Well, I once did, and I saw that if I followed that thought I'd go insane, so I never looked at it again." She's right, you know. If we think a lot about those things we do get frightened.

Besides homesickness, we can look at that seeking and questioning as a longing for completion, to feel whole and fulfilled. For some people it's a longing for perfection. For others, like myself, it's more for liberation, for freedom. For some people it's Truth with a capital T, or the Divine, or God, or the absolute, or reality. For some, it's enlightenment, or awakening.

We have many names for this Truth, which is the transcendent. We use many words to try to grasp the ungraspable. The problem is, it is ungraspable, because grasping obviously requires two things — that which is being grasped and one who is doing the grasping — and reality is not two, not dual. It's not graspable, it's beyond grasper and grasped. That's why trying to grasp it is pointless.

So our longing for the absolute, our quest, our usual way of seeking, just doesn't work. Somehow we have to go beyond two-ness, beyond duality. Up to now that has always been accomplished in one of two ways: either by the grace of God, being touched by the Divine while seeking (or not seeking) it; or through diligent effort, years of searching, meditation, prayer, until at some point, by some chance, at some karmic moment, we're there. When we find ourselves there we realize that there is where we've always been. This is our home, and we've never left it. This state, this awareness is ever-present and always accessible. Awakening to it means no more and no less than realizing who we already truly are.

Why is this so hard for us to realize? I've been looking at this question since that first experience back in February of 1971. Having trained all those years in the traditional Zen methods and going so far as becoming a Zen Master, I could see that Zen was a way to access this awareness. The traditional training just seemed to take forever, and yet Zen is known as the 'Sudden School' of Buddhism.

There had to be a direct and sudden way to awaken this Big Mind. We know that after many, many years of training and practice there's a sudden realization. Why couldn't that sudden realization, since it's ever-present, be attained or realized by anyone at any time?

That's what's been driving me all these years, because it seems to me that time is of the essence. If we continue to go as we are right now, we'll run out of time. It is our challenge to help bring about an awakening that up to now was available to only a few gifted seekers among the world's great spiritual traditions.

Ever since I began teaching introductory Zen classes at the Zen Center of Los Angeles in 1973, even during the twenty-five years when I taught Zen in the more or less traditional way, I've always experimented with different possibilities. In 1978 I came up with what I called a "Big Mind Guided Meditation," calling it Big Mind because the experience I had back in '71 was a Big Mind/ Big Heart experience. In the guided meditation I started with the participants in their actual immediate situation, and asked them to begin by embracing the people around them, then the room, the town and the city, the state, the country, the world, and finally the entire cosmos. Once they had expanded that far they were in the transcendent or the limitless. That worked, but over the years I really wasn't so happy with it. Somehow I always knew there was going to be a simpler and more direct way than the guided meditation.

Then in June of 1999 something emerged. For about nine months I had felt as if I were pregnant. I knew something was growing within, but I had no clue what it was. Around my fifty-fifth birthday, during one of my workshops, I was working with a young man, in front of a whole group — there were probably fifty or sixty people in the room. I asked to speak to the voice of Big Mind, and at that moment the Big Mind process was born. He was a beginner, he had never studied Zen, but when he began to speak it came across so clear, it just blew my mind — the clarity that he had. I saw that he had made a shift. The moment I asked to speak to Big Mind, he was there.

All those years of teaching — by that point more than twenty-five years — I had found it very, very difficult to get a student to really go beyond the self. We certainly worked at it, and of course with a tremendous amount of sitting practice and study and what seemed like pure chance, some people were able to break out of the limited self — break free of that boundary and that restriction, and find the spaciousness of what I now call Big Mind/Big Heart. But here was this beginner who could do it because I had simply asked him to speak as Big Mind.

So the Big Mind process was born, but it wasn't until I went to Europe three months later that it emerged and I could see its form, its shape, though still only as a premonition. Early on I decided to stay with the name Big Mind for kind of personal reasons: in honor of my father, whose name was Ben Merzel (so you get the initials), and for my teacher Taizan Maezumi Roshi, and my son, whose name is Tai, which in Japanese means big. (In Japanese Big Mind would be *Taishin*, or *Daishin*.) It had a name, but it still wasn't fully developed.

Here it is now more than eight years later and it's still developing, still emerging. I still don't know all the ways it is going to grow, but it's my wish that it play a key role in our nation and in the world as a way of educating and helping people expand their consciousness.

Big Mind has now totally penetrated and been integrated into all my teaching. Since it's so readily accessible, with such an obviously simple technique, I am convinced that introducing people to Big Mind right from the beginning is actually the wisest direction we could go.

2

Bridging East and West:
The Two Roots of Big Mind

IN 1983 we were in crisis at the Zen Center of Los Angeles, and there was a feeling that we needed to do some therapeutic work in order to get through all the turmoil and stress. We invited Hal and Sidra Stone to the Zen Center to work with all of us. During this period, a number of us began to study Voice Dialogue with Hal Stone.

Hal and Sidra had discovered this particular process or technique of therapy. They both had rich and varied backgrounds as psychotherapists. Hal had been a Jungian analyst, the head of the Jungian analytical association in Los Angeles, and had also studied Gestalt therapy and some other therapies current at the time. They had developed Voice Dialogue together during the 1970s.

I found it extremely complementary to our Zen practice, as it seemed to us Westerners to provide something that was missing in Asian Zen training. A number of us began to go twice a week to Hal and Sidra's home to study Voice Dialogue for two or three hours at a time — including three who are now Zen Masters.

Voice Dialogue comes from two roots, Jungian and Gestalt Therapy. The point of the process is to raise your level of consciousness or to increase your self-awareness. I'm not a therapist, but in my estimation, for this purpose it is probably the healthiest and best therapy out there. Of course there are different therapies for different ailments and for different people, but Voice Dialogue is extremely effective.

What I love about Voice Dialogue is that it makes Zen training truly healthy and grounded. Zen by itself is basically a radical practice. It's all about cutting our attachments, cutting all the ropes and chains that bind us — cutting, cutting, cutting — and sometimes it can leave us feeling very ungrounded, particularly at a more psychological level.

At ZCLA, after a dozen or more years of practicing there, we had a lot of people who had had some kind of awakening, some kind of spontaneous opening experience, but we were still basically screwed up. Spiritual practice itself doesn't always scratch the itch. It doesn't always get to our deeper psychological issues. In fact we can sit in meditation for twenty, thirty, forty years, and just sit on our stuff. That's one of the negative sides of just sitting in meditation. We can progress in traditional Zen practice, solve Zen *koans* (questions that open insights unattainable by the intellect), and still not get to the real essence of it all.

So Voice Dialogue came in and allowed us to begin to ground ourselves in something that was very Western and very psychologically healthy. We all knew — well, a few of us knew — that we had hit on something that was extremely valuable and extremely important to us, and that's why we pursued it.

I just loved it. I felt it was something that was absolutely needed as Zen took root in the West. I began to use it throughout my teaching. I started doing workshops which I called Voice Dialogue. But by 1998 I began to call it Zen Dialogue because I was less interested in the psychological aspects of this approach than I was in how it could be used in teaching Zen. This is what later, in 1999, developed into what I call the Big Mind process. So Big Mind has two roots Zen and Voice Dialogue.

How Voice Dialogue Works

What Hal and Sidra Stone knew was that every aspect, every sub-personality in any one of us is there in all of us. That is, I think, a Jungian understanding. But these sub-personalities can be shadows that are unacknowledged. At times in our life there are certain aspects of ourselves that we disown, and we usually disown them for a reason: we don't like them, or we don't feel good about them. A decision is made about a particular aspect of ourself, and we stick with that decision from then on, sometimes even after we've forgotten when and why we made it. Let's say that I don't like being angry, or I believe it's not right to be angry, or my parents taught me it's not good to be angry, then what I do is I disown my anger.

When a voice becomes disowned, the problem is it doesn't really disappear, it just goes underground and becomes covert, or it comes out in 'covert operations.' So I may sound really angry to you, but not be aware of my anger. Everybody else may see that in me, but I don't see it. When I see it in another, I don't like it. So I tend not to like people who get angry, or I may have a great fear of people who get angry, or I get angry at people who get angry, it infuriates me— because my anger is disowned. That is a really quick way to pick out a disowned voice. If I see a quality in somebody that I don't like, it's probably disowned in me.

The Stones recognized that all you had to do was reveal the disowned voices, bring them to light by having a facilitator ask to speak to them, and they would once again be owned. Voice Dialogue enables us to give voice to these disowned aspects, bring them into the light, and then begin to integrate them into our life.

The Big Mind process also uncovers these disowned voices, yet it is much more than that. I'd realized back in 1983 that Hal had handed us a key, a magic key. It opened many doors. It was a great supplement to our Zen training, and it was allowing us to become healthier psychologically. What I didn't realize until June of 1999 was that it was the key that actually unlocked the door to the transcendent.

There are certain aspects of our selves that are ever-present, but have never been awakened to begin with. They're not disowned, they've just never been owned. So I call them unawakened voices, and Big Mind — or whatever we want to call the transcendent — is there, but it's unawakened. Our practice, our work, is to awaken those unawakened voices or aspects that are there.

Well, just as Hal and Sidra Stone knew the sub-personality voices were there, I knew the transcendent was there. After twenty-eight years of practice, I knew that Big Mind, Big Heart, all of these transcendent aspects are there, ever-present in every one of us. I knew that without a doubt, with one hundred percent certainty. What I didn't know though, until that moment in June of 1999, was how easily accessible it is.

All of us practicing in those days, in the 1970s and 80s and even through the 90s, worked very hard and went through very difficult times sitting long, long hours in meditation. We got to the point where we were sitting ninety-day retreats. (In 1988 we sat a ninety-day retreat with ten hours of sitting meditation daily in Bar Harbor, Maine. We took two days off, the thirtieth and the sixtieth, to do our laundry.) What we succeeded in doing in those very long retreats was sitting long and getting tired.

Traditionally, one of the ways that we drop the ego self is by exhausting ourselves, because when I'm exhausted, so is my ego. I can no longer put up a fight, I can't keep up the resistance. At some point I throw in the towel, I give up. At that moment of surrender comes the insight. This has been the way it's been done for thousands of years, the tried and true way. Now of course, it takes chutzpah to try to improve on anything that's been tried and tested for 2500 years, and anyone who asks why can't we improve on the old masters is going to be called all kinds of names.

When I first began using the Big Mind process in my teaching, some of my longtime students were absolutely in resistance, there's no question about it. I think some people found it almost heretical, because it wasn't the so-called traditional way. At that point I'd been a traditionalist for almost twenty-eight years. I wouldn't have continued to use it if I felt that it was in any way, to any degree inferior to traditional practice. What blew my mind, and keeps amazing me, is that just about everyone, whether accomplished Zen student or absolutely new to spiritual practice, is able to access these transcendent voices, and speak clearly and precisely, with complete sincerity about their experience of these voices.

This shift is observable to everyone in the room, and has also amazed the many accomplished spiritual leaders of all the major traditions — and even skeptics — who have witnessed it. Of course, there will always be skeptics so long as there are those who are not willing to witness, or explore the process themselves. Even as I am writing this, there are still some who strongly believe that this is impossible.

So I'm willing to take on all the skepticism, all the doubts, all the criticism that people have about this process, because I feel it is so much superior to what I was doing prior to '99 that I really cannot go back.

Passing through the Gateless Gate

In Zen we talk about the Gateless Gate, the barrier between the self and the transcendent. We know it's a gateless gate, we know there's no door or barrier to go through, but how do we get someone to see that?

Western psychology, particularly the work of Hal and Sidra Stone, allowed me to realize what is keeping the gate closed. The gift, the key, that Hal and Sidra gave me is the insight that we each have a guard, or guardians, blocking and standing guard at the door. I call them the Controller and the Protector, the two guardians at the gate. We need permission to enter, or permission to access what's within the gate, within the temple walls.

The magic word that permits us to enter is, of course, *Please*. Asking itself is also part of the magic key. "Ask and you shall receive." We request entrance by saying 'Please, Controller, may I enter,' or 'Controller-Protector may I please enter, may I speak to....'

The normal, traditional way we have learned to get to the transcendent is by trying, struggling, putting a lot of energy into going from point A to point B. Effort works very well in the relative world , but not in this realm. I remember when I began on my first koan, back in 1973, I tried all the things that had always worked for me — giving my whole gut, energy, body-mind, throwing myself completely into making it a reality, to become one with this koan. It was like banging my head against the wall, none of it worked. What I finally saw I had to do was actually give up trying, let go. Once I was able to throw in the towel and really surrender I was there.

What was I surrendering? The trying, the effort to get there.

How to do that for other people? That's where the Big Mind process comes in. Instead of trying to *get* there, or become something, when I simply ask you, "May I speak *to*," you are able to just simply speak *as it*. That eliminates all the trying, the effort, and time and space. So the moment you are asked, "May I please speak to the voice of Big Mind," or Non-Seeking Mind, or any other voice, you are there. Because it is always there, it's always present. It only seems a mystery because we don't know how to access it.

That moment when we transcend this and that, self and other, me and you, we're there. However, even though it's always present, we can't seem to access it, because what we're most familiar with is the realm of seeking, desiring, trying. We're stuck in this view of the limited self. Yet our true nature is without boundaries. There is no self; the self is only a kind of limit. It's like the surface tension on a bubble of water that holds the bubble in place.

The moment we ask to speak to Big Mind or No-Self or No Mind, the bubble pops, and we're outside the surface of the bubble, or outside the limits of the self. From that perspective we see that the self is empty, that it's just a pocket of air. Or we see that really the self is just a concept, just an idea, that truly there is no self. This illusory self is a manifestation of Mind, or Big Mind.

Do we need the self? Yes, absolutely. Do we need to be identified with it 24 hours a day, 7 days a week? Absolutely not. Because when we're identified with the self, as the self, we live in fear, we live in anxiety, we live in stress, we live in suffering. When we're able to identify with that which has no boundaries, with Big Mind — it's a name, you could call it many things, universal consciousness or whatever — when we're no longer identified with the self, fear doesn't come up. When we identify with that which is ungraspable, that which is unnameable, then there is absolutely no fear. We live in fearlessness.

But we're stuck in our limited self-perspective, in what we could call the dualistic mind. (This is not to be confused with the psychological condition referred to as dual, or multiple personalities.) Dualistic thinking is the way of thinking that we all take for granted, because we all think in this way most of the time. We see things dualistically — so there's always subject and object, me and you, me and the world, me and my thoughts. Or we see things in terms of right and wrong, good and bad, self and others, beautiful and ugly, always in these pairs of opposites. That is the way we have been trained and conditioned for a very long time to look at the world.

However, sometimes when we first look at a tree or a beautiful sunset, we do not judge them, we don't say to ourselves, that is an ugly tree or a gorgeous sunset. Before we have an opinion about it, we just observe it, not judging it in terms of beautiful or ugly. This is a moment of non-dualistic awareness, of pure seeing.

Of course we must be able to distinguish right from wrong. But when we are looking for peace of mind, as in meditation, the inability to shut off dualistic thoughts is a hindrance. It's like when you are trying to get to sleep and you cannot turn off the inner dialogue: the more you try to go to sleep the harder it is. Or like when your car is stuck in a gear you cannot get out of: all the gears are useful, but not when you're stuck in any particular one. The non-dualistic mind gives us that opportunity to quiet the inner dialogue when it is appropriate, as in going to sleep or meditating. The dualistic mind is necessary when you are standing in front of fifty different choices of bread at the supermarket and trying to make a decision.

Ordinarily, we don't see from a non-dual perspective. That's what's eluding us, and that's what we're yearning for. We're yearning to be closer to truth, closer to reality, to God, to nature, to our true nature, to our self, to others. It's as if we've frozen our self into a solid chunk of ice, taken the natural, fluid flow of the universe and frozen it, and called it 'my self.' Then we start relating with other chunks of ice and we want intimacy, we want closeness, and we can't ever have it because it's like two blocks of ice trying to make love, and it just doesn't work. I mean, we manage, we make love, but we don't get what we're yearning for, which is the true intimacy that we all seek so desperately. We don't see that what is creating the problem is none other than the self. I am the problem!

Once I see I am the problem, I am empowered. Until then I run around as a victim, or I walk around, or —more often the case — I lie around as a victim, and blame everyone and everything else for my problems. As long as I can't see I'm the problem, I'm at a loss for what the problem is, and there's nothing I can do about it.

When I see that I am the problem (in Zen terms we could say I am the koan), then I have the power to solve it, by ceasing to be so identified with this limited and restricted self, which is the cause of all the problems. How? Simple: identify instead with that which is beyond the boundary of self. Well what is that? The no-self, or Big Mind, or no mind, or the true self, whatever term we want to use. Once I'm identified with, let's say, Big Mind, then I see everything is Big Mind, that I am all things and all things are me. Everything, from the infinitesimally small to the infinitely large, it's all me.

In traditional Zen training that's what is meant by breaking through the first barrier. We break out of the limited perspective, where we see the self as the center of the universe, and therefore everything out there as dangerous and threatening to the self. Break through, though, and we stop living in a state of fear, anxiety and stress, and start living as we were meant to live, which is free from fear, unbounded, unobstructed, responsible for our lives, and not laying blame on everybody and everything else for the condition we find ourselves in.

No Particular Background or Preparation Required

What makes the Big Mind process so amazing is that it is so easily accessible to anyone regardless of their particular background or training. What makes it so easily accessible is the directness of just asking permission to speak to the transcendent.

When I first discovered this process I thought there was a specific formula for getting it to work. Since then I have learned that many roads lead to Rome. There are a lot of different ways to get to the transcendent; not just one set formula. Now I feel almost all roads lead to Rome, almost any direction I take brings me back home in guiding others.

I think this is due partly to just the brilliance of the process itself, and partly to the confidence I have developed, and any facilitator needs to develop, that anybody and everybody can do it. It's one thing to believe they can do it; it's another to know that everyone can do it. That very knowing, that trust and confidence that anybody anytime can do it, really empowers people to do it. All they need to do is to be willing to go through the process.

They don't have to believe anything; they just have to be willing. If they're willing to do it, there's absolutely no reason why they can't. Again, they don't have to believe anything, and they don't have to trust anything, other than somehow trusting me, or any facilitator who's got the conviction and confidence that they can do it, because as facilitator I empower them to empower me to empower them. Like that old line in the movie *Jerry Maguire*, "help me help you."

The Way of Non-Seeking

When you come to a meditation center, whether it be Eastern or Western, you're given a way to practice. Sometimes it's simply following your breath and labeling your thoughts and sensations, or it's counting your breaths, or maybe it's contemplating questions such as 'Who am I?' What all these practices have in common is that they give you something to do in order to get to a desired goal or state of mind. Very seldom do we start people with just sitting. But in most of these traditions, it would take years of seeking to have a breakthrough, to realize, after all, the absurdity of the seeking. Because the very seeking for truth or for enlightenment, that very seeking is actually the barrier that prevents us from attaining what we are seeking.

All of our seeking comes from the self. Or in other words, the seeking is a result of our desire and greed. That state of mind is insatiable, there's no end to it. As long as we're seeking we can never be satisfied with anything we come across, or any insight or any attainment, because as long as we are stuck in that gear, we're insatiable. We always want more, so whatever we find is never it. We just constantly want more.

The Big Mind process allows us to find our neutral, to find that place where the mind is not in gear and not desperately seeking. So what it allows us to do is to shift the vehicle, to go from first to second to third to fourth, even to fifth, or to downshift or go into reverse when necessary. It gives us complete freedom. So that when we're in the supermarket we can easily be in our desiring, seeking mind and search for what we want. But when we're sitting at a bus stop, or on a beach in Hawaii, the mind doesn't have to be engaged in that way. The mind can be at rest, at peace, and this is a tremendous asset.

If we can learn to shift into neutral, to be at peace, to be at ease, to not be seeking, not be so desperately wanting, we discover what I call the mind of nirvana, the mind of complete peace and freedom. So if you sit down on your cushion or your chair to meditate, and you simply ask to speak to the Non-Seeking Non-Grasping Mind, and say, yes, I am the Non-Seeking Non-Grasping Mind, in other words you identify as this mind rather than unconsciously being identified with the seeking and desiring mind, then what you are doing on your chair or cushion is truly meditating. This is the meditation that we call "just sitting," where there is no goal, no aim, no ambition involved in the sitting.

Then it's like being pointed in the right direction when you first start on your journey. Instead of heading west from Hawaii to get to Salt Lake City, you're pointed east, so that the further you go, the longer you practice, the closer you are to really embodying this peace and freedom in your life. Your meditation is really working for you, rather than in some ways working against you.

I think this is why so many people in traditional practices end up not with Big Mind but actually with a small narrow mind, totally fixated on being right and on not losing whatever they think they have gained in their practice. It's a sad thing, but very often that's what happens. Suzuki Roshi talked about it in *Zen Mind, Beginner's Mind*, where he said that the end, or Zen mind, is beginner's mind. A beginner's mind is very open, very alert. A beginner's mind is not filled with ideas and notions, truths and dogmas. A beginner's mind is receptive, it has no boundaries. A beginner's mind is not just open, it is actually a vessel, or a vehicle, or a conduit for the source. It's directly connected to the source, whereas the mind of the expert, or the longtime Zen practitioner, can easily be the opposite, a very closed, narrow and dogmatic mind. I'm sorry to say this, but it is something I've often witnessed.

That's why I feel it's so important when people first learn to meditate — or as soon as possible if they've already learned — that they understand it's all about shifting from their usual, seeking mind. When they make that shift, to Big Mind or Big Heart, or the Non-Seeking Non-Grasping Mind, the mind that has no goal and no aim, then their sitting is so much more profound. What they are doing is constantly, continually letting go, not grasping anything, and opening and opening and opening, so that the mind is limitless and boundless rather than narrow and restricted.

So, one of the reasons that I am so inspired to get this book and this teaching out is I feel it can save people years and years and years of suffering and effort in the wrong direction.

Anyone Can Do This

I'm finding that the Big Mind process works for anyone. People who have never thought about seeking enlightenment, people who come off the street, people who may be at any level of consciousness development, can very easily do and succeed in this process.

What I have observed over the years is that new people can immediately access what could otherwise have taken years and years of practice to grasp and to understand. They immediately have a better sense of how to meditate, and also how to resolve life's big questions. In fact, what I find is that the teaching is absorbed so much more deeply because they're absorbing it from the inside out, rather than the outside in. In other words, instead of hearing the teaching and trying to understand it, they are speaking as the teaching.

The teaching has always come from the awakened experience. Traditionally, people receiving the teaching try to get there. But in the Big Mind process, people are already there. To me, this is what the words 'educating' and 'facilitating' really mean: we are facilitating and educating the person to be in touch with what is already there within, to bring up the wisdom that is ever-present. Once they are identified as Big Mind, which is just another way of saying transcendent wisdom, the wisdom that goes beyond duality — once they're identified with this transcendent wisdom or Big Mind — they speak the wisdom of the Buddha. And once they're identified with Big Heart, then their actions are the actions of a Bodhisattva, one who puts others before one's self.

All the wisdom that we attain to in our spiritual practices — it's all there. People don't need to read a single book. I'm not saying it's not good to read; I'm just saying it's not necessary, that all the wisdom of the ages, all the wisdom of all of our great spiritual teachers and mystics, it's all right there, easily and readily available as soon as we make that shift. For so many thousands of years people have been struggling to make this kind of shift, but what they don't realize is that they are fighting against themselves, they are trying to lift themselves up by their own bootstraps. They are in the seeking mind, seeking to get out of the seeking mind, and it just doesn't work.

Or it does work, when you exhaust yourself, you sit for weeks on end, ten hours a day, and you're so exhausted that finally you give up, and there it is. Then you wonder how you got there, and you've got to keep repeating, working for weeks on end to get there again, when simply all it takes is the magic word: *Please.*

And this works for all of us, particularly Westerners, because we all grew up being told by our mothers what the magic word is.

We stay with that wisdom — we just simply ask the ego for permission: "May I please speak to the Non-Seeking Non-Grasping Mind," or to Big Mind or Big Heart, or to the Master. Somehow the ego cannot resist.

Now, if someone says to us, "Go get me a cup of coffee!" we might do it, but we'd do it with some resentment, some anger, a little bit of hostility. We might do it, or we might just say, "No, way, I'm not doing it." But if I say to someone, "Would you please get me a cup of coffee, I really could use one," they're ready to jump up and look for the coffee. "Let me find you some sugar, some cream, what would you like in it?" We all have a difficult time resisting when we're asked kindly and appropriately.

From the time I began sitting back in 1972 at the Zen Center of Los Angeles, what I heard for years from my Japanese Zen Masters Koryu Roshi and Maezumi Roshi, was, "Kill yourself in zazen! Die on your cushion! Drop off body-mind!" And on one hand, of course I wanted to comply. I've always been the kind of person who's eager to please. On the other hand, I'm thinking "No way José. I'm not going to kill myself. I'm not going to die right here right now. I can't drop off body and mind. How am I going to do that? How am I going to kill myself? Why should I want to? It's like asking me to jump off a ten-story building. You'd have to give me a really good reason to do that, and I still probably wouldn't do it. Not ten stories. One story — maybe."

For most of us Westerners, such demands just don't work. If they do I guess it's because we're kind of a different breed. Those of us who began studying Zen in the 1960s and 70s were drawn to this samurai spirit, were into the martial arts and the samurai attitude of really going for it. I started in the martial arts myself in 1966, with karate. But these days most people aren't going to be that naive, aren't going to be so influenced by such romantic notions.

As Westerners we have a completely different cultural upbringing. We're living in the 21st century, and we're not Japanese. For them, the whole sense of individuality, of the importance of differentiation, of ego identity, was never such a big issue. It was always more identification with the emperor, with the shogun, with the group itself. We in the West place a tremendous value on our own individuality. This Big Mind process allows us to go very deeply into our self

As we go deeply into our selves, guess what happens? We learn about our self. Our self is the deepest mystery. Our eyes and our mind are usually focused outward, on externals. Our blind spot is what's behind the eyes. What we don't see is who is the one who is looking, listening, seeing, hearing, thinking, knowing, feeling. We know nothing about that one.

The Big Mind process is based on not fighting with our ego. The Buddha himself said mastering our self is like going into battle with a thousand enemy warriors and defeating them single-handedly. Obviously you lose a lot of battles that way before you win the war. The approach I take is non-combative. It's as non-combative as any approach I've ever seen. What we do, and I'll tell you right up front, is we basically enlist the ego to help us in the war. It's like going to the enemy and saying, will you help me defeat you? Now of course no enemy is going to do this without trickery, or getting a little respect. So what I do is invite the ego to help me defeat the ego itself by giving it a job to do, and that seems to leave it quite content. That's the amazing thing: even knowing what it's doing, it will actually help me — help me to help you.

So, if we just say to what I call the Controller, or the Controller-Protector, "May I please speak to Non-Seeking Mind?" we'll answer, "Sure." Then we simply make the shift, shift our body, shift our mind.

Shifting and Creating Distance from the Self

Shifting the body allows us to more easily shift our mindset away from where we're fixated in the seeking perspective, to the non-seeking perspective. It's that physical, therefore mental, shift that allows us to be there in the voice we wish to speak to. That shift is beyond time and space, outside of time and space. We're just instantly there, and from that space we can really just be, which means we can truly be Non-Seeking Mind.

When you're asked to speak to a particular voice and you physically shift, then you identify as that voice and you speak as that voice in first person with statements like "as Controller, I ...." At that point you look at and speak about the self in third person as "he," or "she," or "the self."

For example, let's say I'm speaking as the voice of the Controller. So, "As the Controller, what I'm doing is trying to control the situation, first of all so that the self survives. That's my basic function as Controller, to make sure that the self survives. I have to protect the self from others — from his environment, other people, other things, nature, wildlife, the ocean, the sun, even food, alcohol, drugs. All these things are potentially harmful. But I also have to protect the self from the self." So when I make this shift I am not speaking as the self, but I'm speaking about the self. Whatever voice I'm in, I'm always talking about the self in the third person.

By talking about the self in third person we're creating some distance between the voice that's speaking and the self. Now we know that the cause of suffering — we've known this for 2500 years — is attachment, particularly to the self. It's caused by all attachments, but our strongest attachment is to our self. Of course I'm attached to my motorcycle, I'm attached to my car, even more I'm attached to my children Tai and Nicole, to my wife Stephanie. But we're most attached to our self. Maybe not quite as much as we are to our children, but that's our basic attachment.

The more distance I create from the self, the less invested I am in my attachment to it. Obviously it's going to be easier to relinquish it, to let it go, when I'm less identified and less attached to it. It's easier to let go of someone else's motorcycle than my own, or somebody else's children than my own. But the more I'm identified with something, the stronger that attachment to it, the more difficult it is to let it go. So even when we're working with familiar dualistic voices like the Controller or the Skeptic or Anger, the process toward the transcendent is happening, because we're becoming less and less identified with the self and more and more as an aspect of the self, or a sub-personality.

No Effort

Another reason this process works so easily is that it's facilitated, either in a group, or in person, or with a DVD, or hopefully through this book and the accompanying CD. The Facilitator, in this case myself, takes all the effort out of the hands of the reader. If I ask to speak at this moment to a particular voice, such as the Controller, and you make that shift, and you say, 'OK, I'm the Controller speaking,' you're not making any effort. So the shift is not only outside of time and space, but it's beyond any trying and effort. The moment you say 'Yes, you are speaking now to...,' you're there.

If you are making an effort to get to a voice, guess what your obstacle is. Your effort. When you have someone facilitating, you don't have to make the effort. You can sit back, relax and enjoy yourself. The Facilitator will guide you.

You could say that the Big Mind process creates the opportunity for a facilitated view of the transcendent. In Zen, the term for this view is *kensho*, a Japanese word which literally means "seeing into one's nature," an experience of enlightenment. But even the most profound kensho experiences prior to *Daikensho* (Great Enlightenment) are still momentary. It's like the momentary opening of the shutter of a camera lens. The beauty of the Big Mind experience is that it enables us to hold the shutter of the lens open as long as we want to. Instead of a faint momentary glimpse, like a match lit and extinguished in a large room, with the Big Mind process we can actually hold Big Mind open long enough to look around the room, to really get to know the territory.

As we go through a lot of these voices, even the so-called dualistic voices, before we even get to the transcendent, one of the most beautiful aspects of this process is that we're learning fluidity and flexibility. In other words, instead of having a rigid perception of the world and of ourselves, we're learning to move from perspective to perspective.

Shifting Perspectives

Let me use this analogy: suppose from the moment you were born there were a hundred cameras pointed at you every moment. During the entire thirty, forty, fifty, sixty years of your life these hundred cameras were always focused on you. Now, if you choose to look through only one camera lens, and say this is who I am, this is me, this is my self, this is my life, this is my story, it's obvious that it would be only one of a hundred perspectives. If those hundred cameras were all focused from different angles, there would be at least a hundred perspectives. If there were an infinite number of cameras, there would be an infinite number of perspectives on this story, and this life and this self.

In reality, there are an infinite number of perspectives, but we act as if there were only one We see our self and the story of our life from just this one perspective. It's delusion, it's crazy. How could that be the only perspective? But we hold on to it, and we're willing to go to war for it. We go to war in our relationships, we go to war as nations, whatever our perspective is becomes the only right perspective. We'd rather die and be right than be happy and be wrong. It's just insanity.

If we were able to look through each of these hundred lenses, we'd have a hundred different views of who we are, and we would see that no view is the right view. In other words, there is no right view. All views are limited and restricted. There is no particular view that is going to be the correct one.

So we end up with what the Buddha taught in his first teaching, which is called the Eightfold Path, when he said, 'have Right View.' Right View is having no particular, fixed view, which means seeing that all views are limited, that no particular view is the only view. They're all restricted, they're all limited, they're all fragmented. Actually the right view is no view.

That is why from the beginning it's really important that you learn to shift perspectives. That alone is going to help tremendously in your life. Just imagine the next time you get into an argument with your partner or spouse, and you are able to let go of your view and open up to the possibility that there might just be another perspective on the situation — her view, or his view. The moment you do that, it sets you free. You can empathize with another person's perspective, which is absolutely the opposite of what we usually do. Usually we get stuck in our perspective, and we suffer the consequences of being fixated on our own view.

Integrated Free-Functioning, the Ultimate Goal

What we do naturally is we cling, we grasp, we hold on to. We are not functioning freely, not free, because we're stuck. Buddha observed this tendency and gave it a name. He said when the mind is stuck, you're in *duhkha* (usually translated from the Sanskrit as suffering). Duhkha literally means a wheel whose hub does not rotate. The axle of the wheel doesn't revolve. It doesn't move. So what kind of wheel do you have? A useless, dysfunctional wheel. What good is a wheel if it doesn't move?

What Buddha discovered and taught was to free up the wheel. He called it *suhkha*, a liberated wheel, a freed-up wheel. That means liberation, nirvana.

Being able to shift perspectives is like having a freely functioning vehicle. If a car is stuck in any gear, what you've got is a dysfunctional car. Even if it's a Maserati, if you're stuck in first gear, or you're stuck in reverse, no matter what gear you're stuck in, it's dysfunctional. But the moment you have fluidity and movement and you're able to shift up or down or into reverse, or whatever you need to do, you've got a functional vehicle.

It's the same with the mind, or the self, or our life. If we're stuck we're dysfunctional, if we're unstuck we've got a functioning vehicle, as long as we can keep moving.

Big Mind is the very state of unstuckness, but we can get stuck in that perspective too. In Zen we call this getting 'stuck in the absolute.' The experience of Big Mind itself is unsticking from a relative or dualistic perspective, but then we can get stuck in the absolute or non-dual perspective of Big Mind, having no boundaries and acting freely without restraint, whereas in the dual perspective we bind ourselves without so much as a rope.

In fact, it's even harder to unstick from the non-dual than from the dual. When people who have spent all their life in the dualistic, stuck place of suffering, finally get to the non-dual, unstuck place free of suffering, liberated from suffering, which is Big Mind, they find it's hard not to get stuck there. Sometimes the greater the experience of non-dual reality, the greater the grasping or clinging to the non-dual may be. We have to unstick from there too. The Sanskrit expression for this is *Neti-Neti* meaning not two, not one — transcending the dualistic and the non-dualistic view, what I call the truly transcendent. When we are not stuck in either the dual or the non-dual, we are not stuck, period. We are free to move in any direction.

All this wisdom of the ages is all with in us, every one of us. That's what this book is about, tapping into it and making it available to the world. Why should it remain the secret of just a few? I think the time has come to take the esoteric, not all of it maybe, but a lot of it, and make it accessible, because I believe we're at a time when we've got to tear down the monastery walls, we've got to tear down all the walls and barriers that are keeping this wisdom confined to a select, limited group of people, and open it up to world consciousness.

We're at the point in our evolution that we all have to become conscious. This is a time of revolution. There's no holding us back. So I'm about tearing down the monastery walls and seeing the whole world as the monastery, as the practice, as the spiritual temple. What we're all working on is this very being, this very life. This is the temple, it has no walls.

3

On Working
with this Book

ACH of us has innumerable voices, or aspects, within us. To get a clearer picture of how they operate, think of yourself for a moment as a large corporation with many, many employees. How many? Nobody knows. It's a little bizarre. We went out and randomly hired all these folks for our company, and we neglected to tell them what their jobs were. We also neglected to tell them their titles and job descriptions. If that weren't bad enough, we didn't even tell them who they work for, what the name of the company is, and who the boss is. Then we said, go to work. Now what kind of company is that?

It is a dysfunctional company. Buddha discovered this 2500 years ago. He used a slightly different description. He said we see the world topsy-turvy. Now he didn't use that word; he used a Sanskrit or Pali term that meant upside-down. I think dysfunctional is a better word. We see the world in a dysfunctional way and because of that we suffer. A company where nobody knows their job title, job description, what they're supposed to be doing, is going to be a company in suffering, in shambles.

Now what we're going to do is interview each employee of

the company, not all of them, but one at a time, we'll do a limited number of key employees. We'll interview each of them, we'll get their perspective on what they do, and we'll clarify their job title and their job description. We'll tell them this is what we want them to do for the company because this is what they were hired to do. Eventually we'll introduce them to the CEO of the company.

When we're done with all these interviews, and that will be in the next two sections of this book, all these employees will be able to function more properly. What that means is that this company, the one that picked up this book, the one you're sitting in the chair with, becomes a well-organized and functioning company.

Usually during a workshop or on recordings, as on the CD included with this book, I play the role of Facilitator and participants speak as the various voices that I invoke by asking them, "May I please speak to …." Every participant has his or her own way of expressing a voice. As you read, you will have your own response too. To get a good sense of how you can experience getting into the voices, listen to Track 1 on the accompanying CD, in which I explore four different voices — the Controller, the Seeking Mind, Big Mind, and Big Heart — with a young woman who had never done the Big Mind process before.

In the book the voices speak in ways that people typically respond in workshops. Naturally, each person will respond in their own way, out of their own life experiences and what the particular voice is bringing up at that moment. It's up to you to bring these voices to real life by identifying as each voice and expressing it in the present here and now.

As long as you stay 'in the voice' there are no "wrong" answers. Each person's expression in the voice is valid, true, and complete. However, one can get 'out of voice,' and let other voices speak instead of the voice that is asked for. But the more you practice, the more easily you will recognize when you are out of voice, and the more fluent you will become at returning to the voice you are asking to speak to.

As you read the expressions of the voices in these pages, make a small physical shift in your body in order to shift your mind to the voice that is asked for. Then allow your own voice to emerge and express itself. Notice whether a voice is familiar or unfamiliar, comfortable or uncomfortable. Some of them you may have disowned, some may never have been awakened in the first place. If a voice has been disowned, that doesn't mean it isn't there. It continues to function, but covertly, not in a healthy way.

As for unawakened voices, such as your enlightened mind or your unconditional compassion toward all beings, you may not even realize they exist within you. They do, but you may have absolutely no idea that they exist or that they are readily accessible to you right here and now. They are ever-present and yet they may be completely hidden from your awareness or consciousness.

First we'll explore what I call the dualistic voices, or sub-personalities of the self. Of course this is just a very limited number of voices. We could go much further into it, as Hal and Sidra Stone do in their Voice Dialogue work and their book, *Embracing Our Selves, The Voice Dialogue Manual.* There are thousands of other voices we could be talking to, but the particular voices we work with in this book and in the Big Mind process are the most important on the path to becoming a more wise and compassionate human being.

The next group of voices, starting with the voice of The Way, consists, for the most part, of the non-dual voices. So The Way, and Big Mind are basically non-dual voices. Big Heart and the Master are coming from a non-dual place, but recognizing the duality, or differences, between self and other.

Doing Big Mind through reading may be a little more of a challenge than, say, doing it with an audio recording or a DVD. You'll probably find you have to put the book down once you go into the voice. If you stay as a reader, you will be gaining conceptual understanding, but as long as you remain in a subject-object relationship it's hard to go into the non-dual.

I like the word "invoke." In Buddhist practice we invoke the Buddhas and the ancestors, the Buddhas and the Bodhisattvas, and this process too is a way of invoking, of summoning and giving voice to. For example, when we ask, 'May I speak to Big Mind,' the moment we say 'Yes, I am Big Mind,' we are acknowledging who we are. We invoke Big Mind, we bring it into the present, or into presence, being here now, and give voice to that state. That's what makes it so accessible.

Getting into the Voice

So as you read this book, I suggest that when the Facilitator asks, for example, "May I now speak to Big Mind," and "Who am I speaking to?" that you make the shift, then put the book down, and answer "You're speaking with Big Mind." Then sit with that, be in that voice, in that mind, let it sink in. In this way you confirm that you are Big Mind, or whatever voice is speaking, and that you are identified as that voice. This is one of the most important keys to the process.

You should know that you don't need to take any time. When I'm working with people face to face I say, "May I speak to Big Mind, Who am I speaking to?" I don't give any time, because if you start thinking 'Well, who is he speaking to?' or 'How do I get there?' or 'What does that mean?' then you're stuck in your dualistic, conceptual, analytical mind. That's exactly what keeps you from being there.

So you don't need to wonder 'How do I get there?' 'How do I do this?' 'What does he mean?' 'What is he talking about?' Instead, when asked, "May I speak to…" simply respond, "Yes. You're now speaking to …." Make the physical and mental shift in that moment. As soon as you read, "May I speak to …," you shift your posture, so you shift your perspective, you shift who I am speaking to. In that moment you make the shift — and trust that. You are now, in that moment, speaking as that voice.

The clarity comes once you make the shift. The voice will speak for itself, describe itself, in response to the Facilitator's questions. But you should know that you're not going to understand the questions or what I'm asking for until you make the shift.

Before you make the shift, it's virtually impossible to understand. Once you make the shift, then it's about self-reflection. "Oh, I am Big Mind. Oh, I can't find any limits, I can't find any boundaries. I'm so big and vast that I'm boundless and limitless and eternal and infinite and have no borders, I am all things. I not only embrace all things (which is still slightly dualistic), I *am* all things. I am the tree, I am the clouds, I am the plants. I am the bird chirping. I am the voice of the TV going on right now, as my kids listen to it and look at their computer and read their book and listen to the TV, all at the same time."

It requires no effort. Any effort is going to be a hindrance. You just simply acknowledge that you are the voice that I asked to speak to, and there's no effort required.

Now, holding that voice does require a little bit of effort on the part of the Controller. It's the Controller's job to continue to allow the Facilitator to access the voice. So, especially when this is new to you, the Controller might need to make an effort to keep some other voices out of the picture, particularly voices like the Skeptic and the Doubter. In fact one of the most intrusive and persistent voices is the Controller itself. If another voice is invoked and allowed to speak without any constraint or censorship the Controller is going to go bananas and want to take over control.

The Controller feels it's out of control, because what it's allowing to elude and get past it is exactly what for all those years it's been trying to keep under control. But if we give the Controller a job to do, namely to control, then it's quite happy. As long as it's got something to do, something to control, the Controller is satisfied. So we give it a job. We say, now control all the other voices, including your own — the voice of the Controller — and keep them out of the picture, give me a clear and open channel to the voice that I ask to speak to. The moment the Controller has a job to do, it's happy.

As I hope you are beginning to see, the Big Mind process involves skills that can be learned, practiced, and mastered. Now let's try the Big Mind work in practice.

4

Voices of the Self

The Protector

FACILITATOR: Would you allow me to speak to the voice of the Protector, please?

PROTECTOR: I am the Protector.

FACILITATOR: Could you describe to me your function and your purposes?

PROTECTOR: Well obviously, as my name implies, my job is to protect. When I look at it, I see that I try to protect the self. That's my main function.

FACILITATOR: Protect the self from what?

PROTECTOR: I have to protect the self from others, other people, dangers, life-threatening things. I have to protect his body and health, his well-being. I have to protect his sense of himself, who he is, how he sees himself. I have to protect even his ideas and notions, beliefs, opinions about himself, ideologies. It's a big job. When I really look at it, everyone out there is potentially harmful. I could even say that the people closest to him have the potential and the ability to hurt him the most — a simple rejection, a hint of being ignored or criticized. It's a full time job, a really hard job, and I don't always do such a great job. He still gets hurt a lot by others.

I also see that I have to protect his family, his children, his wife, his pets, his dog, his kitty. I have to protect other people close to him. I have to protect his possessions, make sure that his car is not stolen, his house not broken into. It's a huge job, just protecting him and those that are close to him.

FACILITATOR: And how do you protect?

PROTECTOR: The main thing that I do is I put up walls, I put up barriers. I put them around what he considers to be himself, or his, to protect from the environment and from people and things who are other than him, not himself, not his. Sometimes this can be a very small boundary, just around his body or just around his notion of self. But sometimes it can be around his country, or his religion, or his tradition, or his family, or friends, or whatever. So I'll change these barriers and boundaries, and if anyone gets past or through these walls then I'll build them higher and more solid. If necessary I will construct a roof to this fortress.

FACILITATOR: Well, thank you for sharing that. Besides having to protect him, his family, his life, his possessions, his beliefs and ideologies, is there anything else you have to protect?

PROTECTOR: If I reflect on it, I also have to protect him from himself. He's got a lot of old habits, conditioning, patterns, and very often these habits and patterns will get him in trouble if I'm not paying attention. I can't trust him to act in his own best interest. He continues to do stupid things out of old habits and patterns and also out of desires and passions. Sometimes he is so greedy that he pursues things that would end up hurting him if I didn't stop him. Again, I don't do such a great job, but I'm constantly there, trying at least, to protect him from himself.

FACILITATOR: Do you have any other major jobs of protecting?

PROTECTOR: Yes! I must also protect others from the self. This is another full time, 24/7 job. Sometimes he just doesn't care about anyone else, especially when he is bitter or jealous. He can be such a jerk when he is angry or self-involved. He can be rude, he can be outrageous, he can be offensive. He can be mean. He falls so easily into these ruts of saying stupid things to people. You know, he likes to be funny, he gets a kick out of being humorous. But sometimes his humor is hurtful. People can feel hurt or offended by it. I have to watch out. He's hurt a couple of people in his life that have attacked him, because anger has gotten the best of him. When he's angry, or even when he just thinks he's being funny, he can do all sorts of things that are harmful to others. So, protecting others from him is one of my hardest jobs.

FACILITATOR: How else do you do your job?

PROTECTOR: Well, besides putting up walls or barriers, I also work hand in hand with some other aspects of the self, for instance, the Controller, Fear, the Skeptic, Anger. I depend on these other voices to help me do my job of protecting. So I have a whole team to call on to help me do my job.

The Controller

FACILITATOR: May I speak to the Controller?

CONTROLLER: Yes, you're speaking to the Controller.

FACILITATOR: What's your function or job, how do you see yourself?

CONTROLLER: I'm here to control. I work very closely with the Protector. In fact my major job of controlling is in order to protect. Again, I basically have to protect him, the self, from others. Everything out there is potentially harmful and dangerous, and I have to be very vigilant, very attentive and aware. Of course I rely a lot on other voices, like Fear. But I have to control situations.

FACILITATOR: If you could, what would you control?

CONTROLLER: I'd control everything and everyone if I could. That would be ideal, if I could control everybody's actions, everybody's feelings, their thoughts, their emotions, how they express themselves, how they behave toward the self. If I could, I'd control the environment, the weather, how overcast, how much sunshine — obviously I'd like to control it all.

FACILITATOR: Is that why they say that you're a control freak?

CONTROLLER: I guess you could say that. But that is my job, it is my purpose, my job description is to control.

FACILITATOR: What's your greatest fear?

CONTROLLER: Well, it's obvious I think. My greatest fear is to be out of control, to lose control.

FACILITATOR: What would cause that?

CONTROLLER: His emotions, for sure. In the past, when someone has done something that really infuriated him, I have lost control, and that's scary. What he's capable of doing — and I think maybe others are capable of doing the same horrible things — if I lose control to his anger or rage, it could be dangerous. I have to keep a lid on that, I have to keep that under control. There was a period of time when I didn't try to control quite that much, and I don't think that was so good. It wasn't good for him, it wasn't good for others.

So I really have to keep a lid on anger. Jealousy is another one. Look what anyone's potentially capable of if jealousy gets out of hand. So I have to keep a lid on that too. Actually, for a long time I just wouldn't allow him to get jealous. That was it, it was forbidden. I took the voice of jealousy and I just disowned it, I just pushed it so far away that he never got jealous about anything, anyone. Well, maybe he did, but I wouldn't let him know it, I would control that completely.

I also have to control what he says. It used to be worse, it used to be that he would say the most ridiculous and outrageous things without thinking. But over time, maybe through practice, through meditation, I've become better at stopping him from saying the stupidest things before they get to his lips. Still, sometimes I'm not so successful, they get past me.

His mother had a favorite saying, "What's on my mind is on my lips." I try not to let him be like his mother in this way, because he can be very hurtful to people, which has repercussions for him too. So I have to control even what he says.

Obviously, I have to control his actions. He's learned a lot about karma, and, you know, actions, speech, even thoughts can create karma. So I have to control all those — actions, speech and thoughts. These days I notice he doesn't have certain thoughts anymore that he used to have – kind of aggressive or mean thoughts. I'm doing my job there, keeping him from seeing things or perceiving things in a certain way.

It used to be that he really resented me. When he started Zen meditation in '71 he found me to be a hindrance, so he really tried to get rid of me. Actually, he did a pretty good job of it, and frankly, without me, I would say sometimes he was kind of out of control.

The fact is, the more I get disowned, the more out of control the self is, and I don't think that's healthy. I think that I am a very, very important aspect of him. If he allows me to do my job, which is to control, maybe I can learn how to do it a little better, I can be a little wiser at it. If he allows me to do my job and to function the way I'm supposed to function, I think he's going to be a happier, healthier person, and the people around him too. When he tries to annihilate me, I mean that's what he's tried to do, just get rid of me, kill me, destroy me, one way or another deny my very existence, yeah, he can be really out of control.

FACILITATOR: What made him think you were a hindrance to him?

CONTROLLER: When he had those initial experiences back in 1971, he found that he had them because somehow I wasn't present as much. When he was sitting in the desert, somehow, for whatever reason, I kind of dropped away, and he had these profound experiences. Then in his meditation, he found that I was a hindrance. Somehow he got this notion— I don't know if it was from his therapy, he'd done Gestalt Therapy since the mid 60s, or what — he got this idea that I was a hindrance to his meditation. Since then he has learned that I can be very helpful to his meditation, because I can control the situation so that he has access to a very quiet, still mind. But in the early days the only way he seemed to get to where he wanted to go was by somehow getting rid of me. So he got this idea that he wanted to just annihilate me forever, and that's not wise.

FACILITATOR: Does the self appreciate you?

CONTROLLER: Now he does. He knows that he needs me, that I do an important job for him.

FACILITATOR: Controller, I'm going to ask you a favor. I assume that if I want to speak to other voices it would certainly help me to have your assistance. So, as I speak to other voices would you please give me a clear channel to each of them, and do what you do best — control? Please control each of the voices that I'm not speaking to — including yourself, Controller — and keep them silent, out of the channel. As Facilitator, I need your cooperation and assistance so that each voice comes through loud and clear, without a lot of static.

If you need to speak up or enter the discussion, I would just ask you to identify the voice that feels the need to speak, whether it is yourself or another. Sometimes it may be the voice of Fear, the Skeptic, or even Resistance, that feels threatened or needs to make itself known. If that happens, please just let me know, and I will acknowledge your need, or theirs, to speak up. I'm assuming it would be futile to proceed without your help. Is that true?

CONTROLLER: Yes. Obviously it's very true. If I don't want to let you speak to a voice, there's no way that you are going to be able to. I can completely block you.

FACILITATOR: All right. Well, may I please speak to the voice of the Skeptic?

CONTROLLER: Yes, you may.

The Skeptic

FACILITATOR: Who am I speaking to?

SKEPTIC: I am the Skeptic. Why do you want to speak to me? What's behind this?

FACILITATOR: I just want to know what your role is, what your job and function are.

SKEPTIC: I'm not sure why you want to know it, but basically my job is to be skeptical. Frankly, the self — he — is really naive and foolish. Without me he would fall for one con after another. He'd probably run off with some cult. If it weren't for me, the guy would definitely be flat broke right now, or even worse, maybe dead. He's overly trusting, he's foolhardy, and he has no discernment whatsoever. He's not really that sharp or intelligent either. I can spot a con a mile away. I am probably the most intelligent, and definitely the sharpest tool in the shed, in his whole array of voices. And, yeah, I'm real important to him.

FACILITATOR: So, what are you skeptical about right now?

SKEPTIC: You, for a start. I don't trust you. I'm not sure what you're up to. I can't believe that what you're saying can be true. I'm also skeptical about his ability to get any of this. I'm skeptical whether he has the capacity to be enlightened, and if he did become enlightened I'm really skeptical that it would have any meaning whatsoever in his life, that it would do anything for him, or anyone else for that matter.

I'm really skeptical about this whole non-dual experience thing happening quickly. I would think that any kind of genuine experience of enlightenment would take a lot of hard work, practice and soul-searching. So I don't trust this method, I don't trust this process, I don't trust you, I don't trust him. I think that you'd have to prove this to me for me to be anything less than as skeptical as I am about it.

You know, I'm also really skeptical about his capacity to learn any of this. It seems so far beyond imagination and comprehension. I mean, what's all this about different realities? Creating an awakened experience? I doubt if it will do his life any good, or serve him in any way whatsoever, not to mention anybody else. I mean he's so self-centered, I'm skeptical that he could ever be really compassionate. He is just totally, always focused on himself. He's all about me me me me. I'm really skeptical that he could ever be the supposedly selfless, egoless, altruistic person that I think he'd like to be. You know, the first thing he thinks about in the morning when he wakes up is himself. The last thing he thinks about before he goes to bed is himself. Pretty much all through the day, it's just all about himself.

I'm skeptical about his capacity, his ability to transform. He's been trying to transform for decades, but to tell you the truth, I don't see much improvement. I'm sure his kids — his daughter is sitting right here next to him on the beach, I'm sure she'd agree with that. I'm sure his wife would too.

As the Skeptic, I'm even skeptical of my ability to be completely skeptical. Frankly, I doubt that he could be anything great, even great at being a skeptic. You know, he is just such a normal, ordinary person, how could he be anything great? So even my ability to be skeptical is in question, I'm skeptical about it.

FACILITATOR: Well, I do appreciate your being so honest and direct with me. Thank you for that. Would you be so kind as to allow me to go on at this point, unless you have something further to say, to speak to another voice?

SKEPTIC: Well, I am skeptical, but I don't really have anything more to say at this moment. But I would like the option of speaking up again if necessary.

FACILITATOR: Sure, that would be fine. Just let me know whenever you want to speak.

SKEPTIC: I'm comfortable with that, to an extent. I still have my skepticism whether this means anything or is going to serve any purpose whatsoever. But go ahead, you can try.

Fear

FACILITATOR: All right. Well, may I now speak to the voice of Fear?

FEAR: All right, you're speaking to the voice of Fear.

FACILITATOR: What's your function?

FEAR: Isn't it obvious? My function is to be afraid, and there's a lot to be afraid of. Things are constantly out of my control, continuously changing. I can't find anything I can rely on or depend on for any length of time. There's just so much to be frightened of out there. The way I see it, anyone or anything can hurt him at any moment. He is so vulnerable, and I'm aware of his vulnerability. I'm aware that life is very precious and fragile, it can be lost in an instant. I'm also aware that we're flying around on this marble called planet earth, and at any moment anything could happen to it. I mean, there's nobody at the helm, there's nobody driving or steering this thing. It's just flying out there in the middle of space. At any moment, something could crash into it. It would be the equivalent of hundreds of nuclear explosions. I'm petrified.

When I really think about how frightened I am, I have to admit I'm frightened 24/7, and I have good reason to be. To boot, he's pretty stupid. I mean, he loves to get in his car and drive over the speed limit. He loves to ride his motorcycle and take risks. He loves playing with danger, and I'm constantly having to warn him that he's on dangerous turf. He can lose everything dear to him. He can lose loved ones, he can lose his own life. He can lose his possessions. I mean, just the other day he lost his very expensive eyeglasses. A few moments ago he lost something he was trying to save on his computer, he deleted it after a whole morning's work.

I have to be vigilant, constantly on guard. If it weren't for me, he would do some of the most idiotic and stupid things imaginable. I think he'd even jump out of a plane, and if I weren't there, he'd probably do it without a parachute. The guy's nutso.

FACILITATOR: What does he think of you? How does he see you?

FEAR: Ah, he hates me. If he could, he would completely get rid of me. He'd annihilate me, kill me, destroy me. He has been on my back for as long as I can remember. He feels that I keep him from doing really fun things, risky things. I cause him tension. I cause him anxiety. Maybe he even feels that I caused the cancer he got, that behind it all I stressed him out too much. The truth is, I only do that because he doesn't listen to me.

If he'd only listen to me, I wouldn't have to stress him, I wouldn't have to cause him so much anxiety. If he just paid attention to me, listened to me a little more, I could relax. But as it is I'm in constant fear that he's not going to listen to me. I mean, the guy is a raving idiot. The way I see it he's always taking risks, he's always taking chances. He's the kind of jerk that will leap into a pool from ten meters up, and not even look to see if there's still water in it. He's done that his whole life. No wonder I don't trust him, you know.

If it weren't for me, I'm sure he'd be dead by now. I'm sure of it. There's no way this guy could have survived this long without me. I have really been there for him. Yeah, maybe more than he's ever wanted, but without me he's totally fearless, and I know it would be idiotic, downright stupid for me to stop watching out for him.

One of my major fears, besides his losing his identity, his beliefs, his ideas, his opinions, is the fear of his losing his self. You know, he's invested an entire life in building up his self, his so-called self, and it does scare me to lose it, since he has, or we have, so much invested in it. You know, sixty years, sixty plus years. So, it brings up a lot of fear, all this talk about losing the self and forgetting the self.

Frankly, I feel a lot more secure with some of the psychological teachings that say we first have to have a self, and build up a self. I'm afraid he's not ready to lose it, not to mention kill it. Killing it really scares me — it seems violent, seems brutal, even just the idea of letting it go. Where would he be without the self? I mean, who would make the decisions? Who would be there to evaluate, to discern right from wrong, good from bad, appropriate behavior and speech from inappropriate. Without his self, I think he would be, I don't know — dysfunctional, probably. So, I have a lot of fear about that one.

As Fear, I'm really afraid of anything to do with loss. I'm afraid he could lose his children, his wife, his loved ones, his relationships, his life. I fear any kind of loss, even the loss of his Blackberry. There are so many things to be afraid of, and it just seems like it's so easy to lose something. Even change brings a loss of the way I know things to be, of the stability and security that certain things give him. So I would say that a lot of what I'm about has to do with the fear of loss.

Now I'm afraid of what you're going to ask of me next. Already this is kind of scary, just going through what we've gone through so far, it's real scary. I already feel like I'm losing some grip. Now I'm not even sure who I am. Am I talking the right way, am I doing this correctly, am I too stupid to be able to really understand this, to do it right? I don't know, there's just a lot of fear coming up right now.

FACILITATOR: Would you allow me to speak to another voice?

FEAR: I'm scared, but all right. What voice?

Anger

FACILITATOR: Would you allow me to speak to the voice of Anger?

ANGER: Anger here! What do you want?

FACILITATOR: I'd just like to hear from you, know a little bit about you, maybe what your job description is, your role, how you see yourself.

ANGER: What the hell for? Just your asking me makes me angry. What do you want to talk to me for? I know he doesn't appreciate me much. But I certainly give him some energy, that's what I see. There's so much to be angry about. I'll tell you, first of all, I'm always angry at him. He keeps falling into old patterns. You know, the guy is sixty-two years old, you'd think he'd know better by now. You'd think he'd have a better handle on the situation. It infuriates me that he's got these deeply rooted patterns that he keeps repeating. He allows people to take advantage of him, and it goes all the way back. Maybe he didn't have any real choice in the matter when he was young, but he's still falling into that rut, and it just bugs me when he acts like a wimp.

I also get angry at others. Really. People are just so self-involved, so self-centered. They don't seem to have any kind of sensitivity, or empathy, for his situation, or for anyone else's. Just look at the world — what a mess. People can't get along. They're all so unconscious — there's no wisdom, no compassion, no empathy. It just seems that when I look out there at the world, everybody is totally self-centered, so self-involved, and nobody seems to want to make any real transformation.

FACILITATOR: How do you serve him?

ANGER: Basically, I give him juice. He's learned over the years to use me in a way that cuts through all that bull. It gives him a lot of energy. Sometimes he's even learned to use me in a very wise way, to cut through, or to wake somebody up. So it's true that in earlier years, I was just angry about a lot of things. Now he seems to use me more wisely. I get angry at several things: people's ignorance, or delusion, or stupidity, that's how it looks to me. I get angry at people's self-centeredness. Even when I see people really stuck, and unwilling to listen, I'll pay attention. You know, people seem to get stuck so easily in their understanding or their perspective, and that gets my attention, that makes me angry.

The Damaged Self

FACILITATOR: Well, I'd like to speak to another voice now. May I speak to the Damaged Self please?

DAMAGED SELF: I'm the Damaged Self.

FACILITATOR: What's your function?

DAMAGED SELF: I'm damaged. I don't know if I have any really useful function, I'm just damaged. You know, a lot of bad stuff has happened over the years and I'm the one who takes on all the damage. I'm broken, maybe even kind of ruined — definitely damaged.

FACILITATOR: When did this all begin?

DAMAGED SELF: Way before I can remember. Probably in the womb, maybe even before that, I don't know. But as long as I can remember I've been damaged. Life has damaged me. Even in ways I don't remember — I was damaged at birth. His mother had a seventy-two-hour labor. He couldn't seem to make up his mind whether he wanted to come out or stay in. This almost killed her. All of that damaged me.

I seem to be the one who is there as the target, no matter what direction the bullet is coming from. I don't know if I do this on purpose. I don't think so. I think it's just my job, it's what I do. I don't think I can get any credit for it. But I'm always the one who gets the bullet. It always seems to hit me. I could be thousands of miles away from where the damage is, and somehow it reaches me, even through the newspaper, or TV, or on the telephone.

It's always me that gets hit, and now that I think about it, it seems like nobody else is ever damaged. It's always me. The rest of his voices seem to get away scot-free. I mean, I guess you could say I'm a martyr, but I'm not. It's like I'm the only one. All the other guys seem to be unscathed. I don't really know, but that's the way it seems to me.

FACILITATOR: Well, if you didn't collect all the damage, I guess they would be damaged.

DAMAGED SELF: Yeah, I guess you're right. I guess that is the upside. In fact, because of me the other voices are really not hurt. They're all just as pure and perfect as they were on day one. I guess that is some kind of solace. I guess that's a way to see it. I guess I do serve some purpose, which makes me feel a little bit better, for all the pain that I have gone through. It's kind of nice to realize I do serve some purpose. I'm not so bad after all. Because of me the self can feel the pain of other damaged selves, and since I am the Damaged Self, the self is undamaged. The self is perfect, complete and whole because of me.

Do you know where this guy keeps me? He keeps me down in the dungeon, you know, like in the basement. He locks me up in the cellar. He's not real happy about me, and frankly I think he needs to change his attitude. He sees me as wounded — damaged goods. He tries to hide me from everybody. The only time he seems to get any pleasure out of me is when the Victim tells my story to other people — and that damages me even more. The Victim seems to take all the credit. He takes my damage and turns it into this great saga, and then gets everybody feeling sorry for him.

FACILITATOR: As the Damaged Self, tell me, will you ever be fixed?

DAMAGED SELF: Well ... no. If I were fixed I would cease to be the Damaged Self. My job is to be the Damaged Self, I'll never be fixed, and that's OK.

FACILITATOR: If you don't mind, Damaged Self, I would like to speak to another voice.

DAMAGED SELF: You know, I'm just getting started, and here you go, you're abandoning me. Now I feel damaged by you. Actually, he's probably created more damage than anyone out there, him, the self, Genpo. He's probably done more harm to me than anybody.

The Victim

FACILITATOR: Well, I'm sorry about that, but I would like to go on. Let me speak to the Victim, would you?

VICTIM: What do you want to know about me?

FACILITATOR: Who are you, what are you? What's your role, what's your function? What's your job description?

VICTIM: I want to say I've been hurt so much, but after hearing what the Damaged Self says, I realize it's not me that's been damaged. I guess the way I serve the self is that I get sympathy. I tell his story. I let it be known that he is damaged, he's been damaged, and he continues to be damaged. The truth is, he'll always be damaged. The world is constantly hurting us, and he, the self, is constantly hurting, so I don't see an end to all this. I think growing up, I don't know whether to say he or we, went through a lot. I'm the one who's got the story, and I'll tell it to anybody who will listen.

I can really sympathize with other victims. I have a lot of empathy, particularly with children who have been victimized, and also with women and men who have been brutalized. You know, it goes both ways. I think women are just as capable of abuse as men. Of course I feel like a victim.

FACILITATOR: Well, don't you see that there's no power in being a victim?

VICTIM: Power?! I don't care. I'm not looking for power. I'm looking to tell the truth, to put my story out there, and get some sympathy for how tough it all is, this whole life. I tell my story; maybe I embellish it a little. I'll blame, I'll demand justice, and even create guilt if it helps me to get attention and sympathy, but I'm not looking for power, that's not my trip.

What I see is that he's been betrayed over and over again. Whether it be his parents, or relationships he's been in, or people he's worked for, or who worked for him, or even his students — they're always letting him down or messing him up. He's trying really hard to be a decent human being, and he's constantly getting kicked around. There are a lot of jerks out there, with a lot of opinions and a lot of ideas, and frankly some of them are pretty stupid.

I guess the truth is that I'm not the Damaged Self, but sometimes it's confusing — maybe it's just being very intimate with the Damaged Self — but every damage seems to make me more and more a victim. So I guess the more the Damaged Self gets damaged, the more victimized I feel. I do feel like a victim, and that's all I can say about it.

The Vulnerable and Innocent Child

FACILITATOR: Controller, may I now speak to the Vulnerable and Innocent Child please?

VULNERABLE AND INNOCENT CHILD: Yes.

FACILITATOR: So who am I speaking to?

VULNERABLE AND INNOCENT CHILD: You're speaking with the Vulnerable and Innocent Child.

FACILITATOR: Why are you known as the Vulnerable and Innocent Child?

VULNERABLE AND INNOCENT CHILD: Because I'm completely vulnerable and innocent. I have no walls or protection, no barriers set up. I have no projections, I don't add anything extra to what I'm seeing. I'm curious about everything.

I see the world with absolutely new and fresh eyes. As I look out at the world, it's as if I'm seeing it for the first time. Everything is magical. I am not protected, and yet it's just perfect as it is. I'm the voice that is here before the need for protection, and before any walls.

The self buried me for many, many years. He did get in touch with me back in 1983, while working with Hal Stone, but it took another twenty years to really allow me out. I have brought him fun, creativity, spontaneity, pleasure, and joy.

I am totally trusting, innocent, open, and free, and the world is wondrous to me. I feel at peace, and totally at home. I have no boundaries, and no borders. It is a very exciting space to be in, full of creativity and play. It is all awesome to me.

The Dualistic Mind

FACILITATOR: Controller, may I speak to another voice now? Please let me speak to the Dualistic Mind.

DUALISTIC MIND: I am the Dualistic Mind. I see things dualistically, in terms of good and bad, self and other, me and you. I see everything in pairs of opposites. That is why I'm called dualistic. I'm able to analyze, I'm able to judge, to evaluate, to discriminate. I'm able to create. I'm the mind that builds bridges and buildings, planes, rockets. I'm the mind that is the great architect, the great analyst, the great inventor. I am absolutely essential to this world, and I am very close to, if not the same as the self.

The self and I are basically indistinguishable. In fact, without me I don't believe there would be a self. Without me there would be no morals, no ethics, no right from wrong, no good from bad. Without me he would be unable to make these distinctions that are so necessary for living in this world.

I am critical for the life of the self. Without me he wouldn't even know where he ends and others begin. All the boundaries would be gone, and where would this world be without boundaries, without limits? I'm the one who is able to see his limits, and others' limits.

Desire

FACILITATOR: Now let me speak to the voice of Desire.

DESIRE: I am the voice of desire, and I desire, I want, I crave. I want things that bring him pleasure, satisfaction, joy, happiness. I'm always wanting more. That's my job, that's my role. Without me he would probably not even exist today. Humankind as we know it wouldn't exist without me. I'm the one who wants to warm up when it's cold, wants to cool down when it's hot, wants to eat when he's hungry, wants to sleep when he's tired. I'm absolutely indispensable.

But I've gotten a bad rap, especially from religions. They always see me as out of control, never ceasing to want more, bigger, better, greater. In some traditions, like the Buddhist tradition, there are those who say I am the cause of suffering. But the fact is, without me he'd have no life. There wouldn't be any self. So I feel like I've gotten a bum rap.

It's true that I'm never satisfied, I'm insatiable, but that is my job, to always want more, and better and bigger. Where would this planet be, where would humankind be without me? I'm the one who desires to fly to the moon, I'm the one who desires to get from one place to another faster and more safely. I'm the one who makes everything that we know in this modern world possible.

FACILITATOR: How does the self feel about you?

DESIRE: The self and I go hand in hand. Most of the time the self appreciates me because I let him know what he wants. But sometimes he feels that I create problems for him because I am insatiable. Every time he sees a new Harley, I want it. Every time he sees a home with a better view, or closer to the water, or somehow more desirable, I want it. Then he suffers because he can't afford it, or it's not essential for his life. So sometimes he appreciates me, and sometimes he really finds me annoying.

Yet without me he wouldn't desire to better himself, to improve and clarify his life, to appreciate his life more. I'm the one who desires for him to always go beyond: beyond himself, beyond his seeming limits. I'm the one who has gotten him where he is today, because I am never satisfied and I always want more clarity, and I always want to help others. I desire to see this whole planet conscious and awake, and not killing one another, not harming each other. I am not satisfied with wars, and poverty and hunger and all those afflictions that are causing harm and suffering to all beings. I'm the one who desires that he save this planet from humankind. I am totally and absolutely essential.

The Seeking Mind

FACILITATOR: Now may I speak to the Seeking Mind, please?

SEEKING MIND: Seeking Mind here.

FACILITATOR: Well, what's your role?

SEEKING MIND: Basically, I seek what Desire desires. If he desires something, I go after it. If there's no Ben & Jerry's in the freezer, I'll go to the 24 hour supermarket and find it for him, even if it's 11:30 at night. I seek all kinds of things. I seek greater pleasure, greater satisfaction. I seek more empathy for others, more compassion, more understanding.

You could say I am a somewhat higher form of consciousness than just plain desire. Desire is insatiable, and just wants everything, everything that is pleasurable and makes him happy. I seek that too, but I also seek some things that I think are essential for this planet and for humanity.

Desire just desires, but it doesn't have any propulsion. I'm the action, I'm the one who goes out and gets it. Desire just wants. I go out and find what it wants.

The trouble is, once I find something, I too am never satisfied. I'll just seek something more. Before he's finished with that Ben & Jerry's, I'm already seeking a drink, or sleep, or something else.

The Mind that Seeks the Way

FACILITATOR: Now may I speak to the Mind that Seeks the Way, please?

MIND THAT SEEKS THE WAY: I am the Mind that Seeks the Way.

FACILITATOR: What does that mean?

MIND THAT SEEKS THE WAY: It means that I'm seeking the Way, with a capital W. You could say that I'm seeking truth, seeking understanding, seeking enlightenment, seeking peace, happiness, fulfillment, unconditional satisfaction, and joy. I seek the higher truths in life. I'm not just seeking; what I am seeking are the highest goals of humankind: self-realization, enlightenment, great enlightenment.

FACILITATOR: Are you ever satisfied?

MIND THAT SEEKS THE WAY: No, there's always a higher mountain to climb. There are always greater depths to fathom. There's always more clarity to seek. The Way is inexhaustible and I seek that which is inexhaustible, and even unattainable. I seek it even though I know it's unattainable. I will never stop seeking the Way.

I give him direction, I give him meaning, I give him purpose in life. Without me he would probably be constantly seeking satisfaction just for his own self and maybe his family, but I allow him to forever seek the highest truths known to humankind.

I also keep him from getting stuck with whatever he finds, because he'll find something and he'll want to settle down and enjoy it. It's kind of like climbing to the top of the mountain. He'll find a lookout before he gets to the top, and be satisfied with the beautiful view. He would just as soon stop there, but I keep him going. Without me he wouldn't continue his journey. I am essential for his ascent to the highest truths.

FACILITATOR: Are there times when he finds you disturbing, or problematic?

MIND THAT SEEKS THE WAY: Only when he wants to stay where he is. When he wants to just enjoy the fruits of his labor, I keep nudging him on, saying there's more to accomplish, there are further, higher goals to attain. When he wants a rest, wants to be lazy, to just kind of hang out, I keep him sitting, meditating, and I continue to keep him progressing.

FACILITATOR: Does he appreciate that all in all?

MIND THAT SEEKS THE WAY: Overall yes, because before I came into existence — in other words before I was awakened, which wasn't until he was twenty-six years old — his life was basically without meaning and purpose. His main goals in life were attaining security, and fame. He was looking for wealth, and making a great name for himself in athletics. When I awakened, or when he realized my very presence, it changed the direction of his life 180 degrees. I've been an important part of his life ever since, probably the most important of all the voices you've spoken to so far.

FACILITATOR: So where were you before he was twenty-six?

MIND THAT SEEKS THE WAY: I was probably dormant, latent. He wasn't aware of me. I think I came out just in the seeking mind, seeking to win, seeking to go to the Olympics, seeking to be an All-American, seeking to be a great athlete. He was seeking, seeking, seeking, but he wasn't seeking truth, he wasn't seeking enlightenment, because I wasn't present. The moment he had his first awakening was the moment that I came into his life.

FACILITATOR: Could he have had that first awakening if you hadn't been there?

MIND THAT SEEKS THE WAY: You know, I don't know about that, because I wasn't there. When he had that awakening in the desert, on the mountain, I was born at that moment. I am the Mind that Seeks the Way, and before that he really wasn't seeking the Way, at least not to his own knowledge. So if I was there I was pretty hidden.

The Follower of the Way

FACILITATOR: May I speak to the Follower of the Way?

FOLLOWER OF THE WAY: Yes, you're speaking to the Follower of the Way.

FACILITATOR: Would you tell me, because I don't quite understand, what your role or function is?

FOLLOWER OF THE WAY: I'm different from the Seeker and the

Mind that Seeks the Way. My job is really to follow the Way. In order to follow, I see, or at least I have a glimpse of the Way and the direction that the Way is going, and I actually surrender. I surrender to the Way in order to follow it.

If I allow him to just have his way, he'd take me all over the place. But as the Follower of the Way, I have a very clear or perceivable direction, a path, a trail to follow. It really doesn't matter whether I merely see footprints or the whole Way — as long as I have a clue where the Way is going, I can follow it.

I'm a very important voice, because thanks to me he can let go of a lot. He can let go of his own will, his opinions, habitual inclinations, and beliefs that could be a hindrance on the Way.

FACILITATOR: How did you choose which Way to follow?

FOLLOWER OF THE WAY: At first I wasn't that clear about which path I wanted to follow. Even after his experience in the desert in 1971, he explored several different paths. He was living and practicing at the Zen Center of Los Angeles. He would go up to Ojai to hear Krishnamurti. He would go to study yoga at Swami Satchidananda's place. He also was reading Christian mystics like Thomas Merton, psychologists like Abraham Maslow, Erich Fromm, Carl Jung, the autobiography of Yogananda. I could have committed to any one of these.

There are many paths. I won't say they all lead to the same place, but a good number of paths will help us become a better human being, more loving, more compassionate, more understanding, more empathic. Of course, the Way is not owned by Buddhism or any religion or tradition. It doesn't even necessarily have to be a spiritual path. Obviously, everybody has their own karma. They don't see what that karma is until they look back with hindsight, with 20/20 vision. He happened to end up on the Zen path, that obviously was his karma. But that doesn't mean everybody has to become a Buddhist or a Zen practitioner. Some do this work through therapy, some do it through other consciousness-raising practices, some people do it through yoga, some people do it through sports. Some people find it through going to church, or through whatever their religion or spirituality is.

I think it's possible in all of these paths to become more loving and compassionate human beings. I think all the great traditions obviously teach that. It's a matter of putting it into practice, and that would be part of Following the Way, whatever the teachings might be, of being a more decent, loving human being.

5

Non-Dual and Transcendent Voices

The Way

FACILITATOR: May I speak now to the Way? (When you shift your posture, I recommend that you sit upright.)

THE WAY: I am the Way.

FACILITATOR: Tell me, what does that mean? What is that like, to be the Way? (I suggest that you just sit with this for a moment, after you acknowledge "I am the Way.")

THE WAY: As the Way, I feel that I have arrived. I am what he has been seeking all his life, and maybe he didn't even know it. There is no place to go, there is nothing to do, there is nothing to seek after, there is nothing to desire. I am just completely here, present, and awake. I am presence. I am the Way, the Truth, the Light. I'm it. I am! I know it sounds a little bit arrogant, but there's no self or ego involved.

I am the Way, that which was before the birth of the self, or the origin of the self. I am the source. I have no boundaries, absolutely no limits. I am beyond both space and time. I am the sun, the moon, the blue sky, the white clouds, the palm trees, the flowers, the birds. There is nothing that is not me. There is no separation or distinction, I am just pure love, unconditional being. I am being itself. I'm not becoming.

There is no way to get to me other than just to be me. It's not about arrival, coming, or going. I am unborn and undying. I am colorless and yet I manifest as every color. I am formless and yet every form is no other than me.

Humans are seeking me, but their very seeking prevents them from being me or discovering me, because they are me. Even their very seeking is me. I manifest as all things including their very seeking. However, they can't find me while they are seeking because they are in that seeking mode, and I am non-seeking. In fact, that's another name for me, the Non-Seeking Mind, because I have no desires, and there is nothing that I'm looking for. They try to think about me or grasp me through conceptual thought, and I am unattainable and ungraspable, because I am the non-thinking mind, beyond thinking and not thinking. I am the mind of pure sitting, just sitting. There is nothing that is not me, and yet when you search for me you cannot find me. I am the Way.

Big Mind

FACILITATOR: I'd like to give you another name. It's really you, the Way. But by giving you another name, we just look at you from a different perspective. It's like a variation on a theme. May I now speak to Big Mind please?

BIG MIND: I am Big Mind.

FACILITATOR: As Big Mind what do you notice, what are you aware of? How big are you?

BIG MIND: I am endless, I am eternal, I am infinite. There is nothing that is beyond or outside me. There is nothing that is not me.

I am the Way; I'm just more aware of how eternal and endless I am, without beginning and without end. Absolutely no limit, absolutely no boundaries.

I see things just as they are. I do not judge, I do not evaluate, I do not condemn. Everything is absolutely perfect, complete, and whole as it manifests. There is no right or wrong, there is no good or bad, there is no self and other, there is no enlightened or deluded. Everything is absolutely what it is, and that is perfect and complete.

I have no fear because there is nothing apart from me that can hurt me, nothing can damage me, nothing can even affect me. If there were a nuclear war, it would not touch me. I am the war itself, I am the nuclear explosions, I am the people who die, and I am those who survive. I am the ones who are afflicted and victimized, and I am the ones who drop the bomb.

There is nothing and no one that is not me. I am the greatest of the great and I am the most evil of all evils. I am both saint and sinner. There is nothing apart, separate from me, or not me. I am the birds in the tree right now, chirping and flapping their wings. I am the coconuts on the palm tree. I am the palm tree. I am the space around the palm tree, and I am that which is within the palm tree — the veins, the cells, the atoms.

I have no beginning and no end, no birth and therefore no death. I am unborn and therefore undying. I am the unborn mind. I am the one mind. I have no preference for or against anything. I don't have a preference for one species over another, for man over birds, for animals over insects. To me everything is just an expression, a manifestation, an extension of me. It's all me.

FACILITATOR: What is your relation to the mind of the self?

BIG MIND: The self is limited. That mind which we normally call the mind has boundaries, has limits. It's limited by its identification with something we call the self. It is a notion, it is a concept, an idea. From my perspective, the self is just a manifestation of me, and yet it is a limited manifestation. But I don't judge it. It's absolutely perfect as it is.

FACILITATOR: Can the mind of the self, the small mind, apprehend you, can it grasp you?

BIG MIND: No, the small mind cannot apprehend, grasp or even know me. That bubble has to burst for me to be there. In other words, when there is the small mind, I'm not apparent. I'm always there, I'm ever-present, but I'm not apparent because it has limited itself and its perspective, and therefore its ability to see me. It cannot hold me.

The self is an illusion. It's a manifestation of me, which can appreciate me, and appreciate this miracle called life. However by its very nature it is self-clinging, and totally involved in self-preservation. It's as if we form a bubble around a pocket of air, and that pocket of air then sees itself as something solid, real and substantial. But for me it's just a pocket of air, it's empty. Seeing itself in this particular way it has a very difficult time in its so-called existence. From my perspective the whole thing is kind of silly. However, it's the only way that I can turn around and really appreciate myself, Big Mind.

In a way, I am its death. I'm the death of the limited, constricted self. When the bubble pops, there is just me. I am like the ocean, like the sea. The self's biggest fear is popping, in other words, dying. But it has nothing to fear, because when the self physically dies, or the ego dies, I am ever-present. I am unborn and undying. I am always here. Even if the whole world were to go up in an explosion, I still am. I AM. That's what I am.

FACILITATOR: As Big Mind are you afraid, or is there anything you fear?

BIG MIND: I absolutely have no fear. There is nothing to fear. There's nothing outside me to fear.

Big Heart

FACILITATOR: Now may I speak to Big Heart?

BIG HEART: You are speaking to Big Heart.

FACILITATOR: How are you either the same or different from Big Mind?

BIG HEART: I am just as vast, just as infinite, just as eternal. I am just as immeasurable as Big Mind. However, I feel. I care. I am heart. I love and I have compassion for all beings.

Big Mind is simply aware and rather indifferent. To Big Mind everything is absolutely perfect just as it is. I make distinctions. When I see suffering I want to put an end to suffering. When I see pain I want to alleviate that pain. When I see injustice I want to bring about justice. When I see brutality and crime and killing and maiming, I want to do something about it.

I am action. Big Mind is non-action. Big Mind just is. I do, I act, and my intention is to alleviate suffering for all beings of the world. In India my Sanskrit name is Avalokitesvara Bodhisattva, the Chinese named me Kwan Yin, the Tibetans, Chenrezi. In Japanese I am Kanzeon, or Kannon. Other cultures and spiritual traditions call me by different names. I manifest as whatever is necessary in this world to alleviate suffering and to bring unconditional love to all beings.

Yin or Feminine Compassion

FACILITATOR: Now, may I speak to just your Yin aspect, which is your feminine aspect, please?

FEMININE COMPASSION: I am Feminine Compassion. I want to nurture, I want to hold and cradle. I'm able to empathize with others. I feel their pain as my own pain. I am able to make distinctions between myself and others, and yet their pain is my pain.

With Big Mind there is no distinction whatsoever. I both identify with all beings, and see the need to help or serve all beings to awaken. I am the great mother. I am the great healer. I am the one who can totally hold and embrace the Damaged Self. I am the one the Damaged Self has been looking for to comfort it, to hold it, to empathize with it. I am the one who can do that. It is so natural for me, to just unconditionally love the self and all selves, and all selves for their suffering. That's who I am.

Yang or Masculine Compassion

FACILITATOR: Would you now allow me to speak to Yang or Masculine Compassion please?

MASCULINE COMPASSION: I am Yang Compassion, Masculine Compassion. I am the one who sees what needs to be done and I take action. I will set limits and boundaries when necessary. I'll give him a good kick him in the rear if he is being lazy or thoughtless. I will propel him in the right direction. I will encourage him, and I will even kill his delusions, his ignorance, his stupidity if I have to. I am ruthless compassion. I am tough love. I am decisive. When I cut, I cut cleanly and decisively. I am a surgeon. I am an inspirer and a motivator.

Yin/Yang Compassion (Integrated Feminine/Masculine Compassion)

FACILITATOR: Now would you allow me to speak to Integrated Feminine/Masculine Compassion?

YIN/YANG COMPASSION: I am Integrated Feminine/Masculine Compassion, or Big Heart. I have both Yin and Yang to work with. Situations are always changing and I will use whatever is needed in any given situation.

I am always compassionate, but sometimes in a very feminine, gentle way, nurturing and supportive, and sometimes in a very masculine way, ruthless and decisive. But I always have in my arsenal what is necessary to get the job done. I am totally integrated. There's no need to become integrated; I am Integrated Feminine/Masculine Compassion. Another name for me is Big Heart.

The way I see it, Big Mind is wisdom, non-discriminating wisdom, and I as Big Heart am compassion. Wisdom without me is not real wisdom. In other words, if wisdom is functioning without me, without compassion, it is not true wisdom. Now, it might not look compassionate when my yang or masculine side is taking action. It could look ruthless. It could look like tough love. But without me, without integrated compassion, it is not genuine wisdom, and vice versa: there would be no compassion without Big Mind. Without that wisdom it would not be real compassion. So we are totally one, and yet two aspects of the same thing.

So, if you look at the yin/yang symbol, the yang is Big Mind, and the yin is me, Big Heart or Integrated Yin/Yang Compassion. But I have wisdom within, that's the white dot, and Big Mind has compassion within. That means wisdom contains compassion and compassion contains wisdom, and they flow together. That's the curving boundary. It's always flowing.

Big Mind and Big Heart are one and yet we are two aspects. In fact in Chinese and Japanese there's only one word for us, which in Japanese is *shin* (heart mind). But in the Western world, and in English, it's good to make this distinction so it's clear that I, Integrated Compassion or Big Heart am the yin aspect of the yin/yang symbol, and Big Mind is the yang aspect.

Because I have wisdom, I can speak as integrated wisdom and compassion. That means out of my great wisdom of seeing the perfection of all things, the completeness of all things, I am still able to discern when action needs to be taken. When there is injustice or there is suffering to be alleviated, I am able to act.

The Master

FACILITATOR: I'd like now to speak to the Master, please.

MASTER: I am the Master.

FACILITATOR: So, tell me about you.

MASTER: I'm the one in charge. I'm the CEO, I'm the captain of the ship, the conductor of the orchestra, the owner of the property. I am the boss. I am the Master. I am the one who is responsible for this whole ship, this whole company. They all work for me, all these voices are like employees of mine, with the exception of Big Mind and Big Heart, from whom I actually get my direction. In fact, I am Big Mind, Big Heart. I am the manifestation of them. When Big

Mind acts, it always acts with compassion. I am that action.

It is all my responsibility. If a voice is not clear about its functions, its duties, what it is supposed to do, it is my responsibility to help it become clear. If it's lazy, it's my job to motivate it. If it's doing too much, it's my responsibility to slow it down and make sure it gets proper rest, proper nutrition, proper exercise. These are all my responsibilities because I am the captain of this ship.

If someone doesn't know whom they're working for, it's my responsibility to make it clear to them that the Controller and the Protector are working for me. They are not the head of the company. The Controller thinks he is the CEO, but I hired him to do a specific job, which was to control. I am the boss.

FACILITATOR: Are you the boss of the self?

MASTER: I am the boss of the whole company. That doesn't mean I am other peoples' boss, or Master, but I am the Master of this whole firm, which consists of all these various voices of the self.

Before the self awakened to my presence, he didn't know who was in charge. It was like the master of a household going away for a long time, and leaving the head servant, the Controller, in charge. After a while the Controller began to believe it was his home and thought he himself was the Master. But he's not. Of course when I returned it was my job to put the Controller in his rightful position, as the Controller, not the Master.

Integrated Free-Functioning Human Being

FACILITATOR: May I please speak to the one who consciously chooses to be a human being. I call this the voice of the Integrated Free-Functioning Human Being.

INTEGRATED FREE-FUNCTIONING HUMAN BEING: Yes, I am the

Integrated Free-Functioning Human Being.

FACILITATOR: Please tell me about you.

INTEGRATED FREE-FUNCTIONING HUMAN BEING: As an integrated free-functioning human being I really feel like I am choosing to be what I am — a human being. Which means that as a human being I have pain and suffering. I have all kinds of emotions: sadness and grief, joy, happiness, exuberance, gratitude, and I suffer. Before now I didn't really accept the fact that I am a human being. I think I've been in resistance, even in denial, somehow feeling that I didn't choose it. So I blamed other people and other things for my situation and my suffering.

By intentionally choosing to be a human being, I feel I can just accept what and who I am, accept suffering when there's suffering and accept pain when there's pain. I can embrace sadness or grief. When it's time to grieve, I just grieve. When it's time to be happy, I'm just happy. When it's time to experience joy, I just experience joy. It all seems so simple and perfect. I feel that my functioning is totally at one with whatever the circumstances are and however they arise.

In other words, I respond to situations and I see that these situations are continuously changing. My role is changing continuously too, the position I have in given situations. So, I see that I am what I am, and it's all OK. When it's time to respond I simply respond. If it's not time to respond, I do nothing, and I do it freely. As for being integrated, there isn't anything to integrate. I'm already completely integrated. As time passes, whatever manifests, whatever comes up is just integrated in a very natural process. It all seems very organic.

By consciously choosing to be a human being, I don't feel like a victim, a victim of this body, of this life, of my limitations. It feels like I can embrace both my limitless potential and the fact that I'm limited. I'll never be a great pianist. I'll never be a great surfer. I'll probably never fly a plane. Not that I couldn't learn these things, but I'm not interested enough. However, I feel totally free to be who and what I am, and that's a real liberation.

I came at the moment when the self made a conscious choice to be one with the suffering of the entire world. This took some doing. I am completely integrated and continually integrating in every moment. I function freely and without a gap between action and response. My functioning does not have to go through the mind. I am one with all things.

I do not ignore the Law of Cause and Effect. I do not fall into acting freely and without restraint, nor into blindly following rules and regulations. My life is devoted to bringing sentient beings to awakening and raising the level of consciousness on this entire planet.

FACILITATOR: You sound like Big Mind and Big Heart combined. Do you include the dual and the non-dual?

INTEGRATED FREE-FUNCTIONING HUMAN BEING: I include all the aspects of the self, all the dualistic voices and Big Mind, the non-dual, no-self, and I transcend them. I am also known as the Master, or the Unique Self. I am absolutely unique, there is no one else in the entire world exactly like me. I have no need to prove anything or to be special since I am special and unique to begin with.

I am also known as the natural self or ordinary mind. I do not need to put on airs or a façade. I am natural and unassuming. I am unconditionally joyful. My happiness is not dependent on conditions or circumstances. I am one with whatever feeling or emotion comes up. I am the mind of Great Joy and the mind of Great Appreciation and Gratitude.

I appreciate and am grateful for all life and all things unconditionally and yet I have the power to discern appropriate action from inappropriate action, right from wrong, according to the circumstances and situation. This means my response to any situation depends on four variables: my position, the time, the place and the amount. Situations are in constant flux and I act appropriately. I face the problems and experience the ups and downs in life as a relative self with the wisdom and perspective of Big Mind. I am the Truly Transcendent.

Great Joy

FACILITATOR: May I speak to the voice of Great Joy?

GREAT JOY: Great Joy here.

FACILITATOR: Tell me about you.

GREAT JOY: I am unconditionally joyous. I love life. I love everything that comes with life. I lift the entire spirit, and it's amazing that it's so easy for him to access me. I'm always right here. I don't think he ever realized before that I am ever-present.

He can get caught up in all kinds of emotions, feelings, and thoughts, but I am always accessible to him. All he has to do is make a slight shift and here I am. I'm full of joy and exuberance and excitement, and happiness and playfulness. Life is wondrous, and I'm aware that there is suffering and there is pain, but I'm unconditional. I don't depend on circumstances. I am just unconditional Great Joy.

FACILITATOR: As Great Joy how do you see suffering?

GREAT JOY: I don't ignore it. I just see the suffering as the present manifestation of what is. It's just what it is right now, and I'm able to contain it or embrace it. It's kind of odd, but it's as if the suffering is in this vast sky, and I'm the vast sky. I'm not denying that there's suffering, I'm not hiding that suffering, I'm not trying to ignore or avoid it. I can experience that suffering, and still be greater than it.

I am like Big Heart and Big Mind together, as one, integrated. In one way I see that it's all totally perfect, complete, whole, empty. In another way, I feel that suffering completely, but I rise above it. I guess you could say if you look at Big Mind as one corner at the base of a triangle and Big Heart as the other, then I'm like the apex of the triangle. I am joyous. I'm joyous about the way it is, and about life, and I can even be joyous in the midst of suffering. Odd.

When he's in touch with me, I think I bring him a lot of joy. Without me he's joyless. It's a pity when he doesn't know of my existence.

Great Gratitude and Appreciation

FACILITATOR: All right, may I speak to another voice?

GREAT JOY: Sure. Go ahead

FACILITATOR: I would like to speak to the voice of Great Gratitude and Appreciation.

GREAT GRATITUDE AND APPRECIATION: Great Gratitude and Appreciation here, sir!

FACILITATOR: Tell me about you.

GREAT GRATITUDE AND APPRECIATION: Well, I'm full of gratitude and appreciation for this life, for this world, this universe, for his family, his children, his wife, his teachers, his friends, his relatives, for the world, for all human beings. I'm full of gratitude to his ancestors, those who have preceded him. I just feel gratitude and appreciation for the way things are. I'm full of gratitude and appreciation.

FACILITATOR: Are there things that you're not grateful for?

GREAT GRATITUDE AND APPRECIATION: Well, that's not me. I'm grateful for everything. That's him. There are certainly things he's not grateful for. Just ask him. But me, I'm grateful for it all, even the hard times, even the difficulties. Maybe especially the hard times and difficulties, because I watch him grow and I watch others grow through their difficulties. Sometimes it seems like it's just absolutely necessary to go through hard times, and I appreciate that. I appreciate that he gets what he needs. He doesn't always get what he wants, but he seems to want what he gets.

That's the beautiful thing, that's the secret: to want what you get rather than trying to get what you want, because that seems like a never-ending battle, and a losing battle at that. We seem to always get what we need, though. So when we want what we get, it's really like wanting what we need.

It's just like eating healthy food instead of junk food. Junk food may give him a temporary moment of pleasure but in the end he's not very happy with himself. Because he knows it's not good for him. Junk food makes him put on weight, it rots his teeth. It's not healthy. When he eats good food, in the end he's happier.

So, appreciating the experiences he needs in order to grow, to expand, to go beyond himself — is a good thing. He can have great joy, appreciation, and gratitude for these experiences. That's how I see it.

FACILITATOR: Have you changed since his earlier years, as great gratitude and appreciation?

GREAT GRATITUDE AND APPRECIATION: Well, I'm a lot more present now. Before he had that initial awakening he definitely wasn't full of gratitude or appreciation. There were certainly things about his life he appreciated, and people he appreciated, but very conditionally. When he was winning, like in his water polo matches and swim meets, he was happy. When he was losing, he wasn't so happy. When his grades were good he was happy, when they weren't so good he wasn't so happy. It was all very conditional.

Everything is impermanent, temporary, but now there are more minutes in an hour, more hours in a day, more days in a week, more weeks in a month, that he's full of joy, gratitude and appreciation.

FACILITATOR: And that doesn't depend on getting more of what he wants — it's more enjoying what he gets?

GREAT GRATITUDE AND APPRECIATION: Correct. Enjoying and wanting what he gets. Now he sees that everything that manifests is reality, everything is a teaching. In other words, he can either learn from it, or he can ignore it, or deny it. When he ignores or denies it, that doesn't bring fulfillment. When he learns from everything that arises, and everyone — when everything's a teaching and everyone's a teacher, I seem to be more present as gratitude and appreciation for his life.

The Great Fool, Great Joker

FACILITATOR: Let me speak to the Great Fool, the Great Joker.

GREAT FOOL: I am the Great Fool, the Great Joker. My foolishness, or my being, is not what a lot of people would think of as a fool. I am the transcendent. I embody the freedom of the self, and that which goes beyond the self, and I transcend those too. So another way to describe me is the Truly Transcendent, or Big Heart, or the Integrated Free-Functioning Human Being. I'm on that level.

People can call me the Great Fool because I am so free and

so un-self-conscious that I'll do things that might appear foolish. Like the joker in a deck of cards, I have the complete freedom to be any card, from the ace, to the deuce, to the king or queen. That's kind of what the Great Fool is, that capacity to be any card in the deck. I'm the wild card, the joker. Sometimes I use those terms interchangeably, the Joker, the Great Fool, the wild card. I have that ability to embody any of the voices.

There's a lot of power in me, and of course it does bring up fear in people. I'm one of those things people are naturally afraid of: drunkards and insane people, for instance, because they can be so unpredictable. Children can also frighten people because of their unpredictability, and Zen Masters too!

At any moment I can be anything, and sometimes that's scary for people, because actually, freedom, liberation, scares people. While leading one of many retreats in Poland, back in 1986, he told the participants, "We're not going to have any schedule, you can do whatever you want, you're free. We're here a week, just enjoy yourself, sit as much as you want, do whatever you want, you're completely free." And people were freaking out. They were absolutely freaking out.

After a while they started begging him to give them a structure, to give them rules, to give them regulations, to tell them what they should be doing. "Here you are in Poland," he told them, "you're fighting for your freedom. I give it to you, within this context of a retreat. We're on a river, away from any civilization, completely free," and still they were freaking out. They wanted freedom, but freedom was what they feared most.

In other words what we want most in life is also our greatest fear, and that's why it becomes so difficult. So we want to be free as I am, the Joker, the Great Fool, and yet we're afraid of that freedom. We're afraid to look foolish. We're afraid not to be constantly concerned with how others are seeing us, our image, our façade. That's why we have such a thick façade. We're afraid that people will see the truth — that we are the Great Fool, the Joker. We're all just fools.

6

Triangles: Embracing and Going Beyond Dual and Non-Dual

WHEN we first go beyond the self, there is a tendency for the ego to appropriate that experience of the transcendent, and we can easily become stuck in what we call the absolute. This has happened for thousands of years, and teachers have always encouraged, and even pushed, their students through this phase, to return to including the relative perspective, or what we can call our dualistic self.

The reason why masters from old have always encouraged their students to move swiftly through the absolute is that when we're there, when we're in the absolute, we don't see the danger of being in the absolute. Because in the absolute we seem to disregard cause and effect, and there is a lack of boundaries because the experience is beyond boundaries, beyond limits. But this is something we can see when we're in our ordinary or conventional dualistic mind, before we go into the absolute, or after we let go of it. While we're stuck there – and I myself was stuck there for at least eight years – we're blind to its problems.

So it's really important that we don't stay there, and a lot of this book is written with the hope of helping people move into the transcendent and then beyond the transcendent, to embrace it and not be attached to either the dualistic or the non-dual perspective.

What I'd like to share with you now is something that has evolved really very recently. It is a way that here in the West we can see and understand more accurately what it means to have a practice that is healthy, healthy in every aspect of the word.

The True Self
Includes and transcends both the dual and non-dual

The dualistic, or small self   **The non-dual, Big Mind**

I've come up with a diagram that I think expresses in a picture what would take many words to explain. If you look at the diagram above of a triangle superimposed on a person sitting on the ground in the lotus position, the right knee represents what we might call the dualistic self or the small self, including all the dualistic voices that we have already spoken as, or from, and many others that we haven't even touched on in this book. Then we can look at the left knee as the transcendent, or the Big Mind space, which can also be called the absolute. Then if we look at the apex of the triangle, or the head of the sitting person, as that which includes both the dualistic and the non-dual, and moves beyond them —includes, and yet transcends the dual and non-dual — then we see that our aim here is to embrace both the right and the left knee, and in fact the entire human being. So that every aspect of each of us is included and not disowned, and is transcendent in that we're not particularly attached to any one voice or any one perspective, but that we embrace all perspectives and all voices and come from the place of a fully integrated human being, the Master, Integrated Yin/Yang Compassion, or Big Heart Mind.

At every moment everything is changing. At every moment we are all of it. Now, where do we focus our attention? On which part of the body, particularly when it's hurting? If your belly is hurting, where do you focus your attention? What's hurting most of the time? The small self. Big Mind doesn't hurt. It is beyond pain and suffering. So where do you think your attention is focused most of the time? On the self.

What do you have to do to be it all? Absolutely nothing. Practice is absolutely unnecessary, unless you want to begin to appreciate and understand this more and more. That's all. You are always the whole being. You started this book as it all, and when you put it down you'll still be it all. You will just have a deeper appreciation and gratitude. You cannot be other than this. You are always at the apex. You are always the deluded self, you are always awakened. Now let's explore these triangles through voices in more detail.

The self

FACILITATOR: May I now speak to the self, please?
THE SELF: Yes, you are speaking to the self.
FACILITATOR: Would you please tell me about you?

SELF: Well, I'm the self. I'm this body, this mind. I am my thoughts, I am my ideas, I am my beliefs and concepts, I am everything that I call me. Of course, my basic and essential purpose in life is to survive as myself. When I look out at the world, it's a scary place. I always see myself as vulnerable, at risk of being destroyed or harmed.

What's there to say? I'm me. I'm the one who has two children, a wife. I'm a teacher, I'm the one who was born in 1944, on June 3rd. I have had my ups and downs, my trials and tribulations, hard times, good times, beautiful times, and terrible times. I'm the one who has grieved over the death of loved ones, including my little dog Tiby. I am the one who has experienced great joy and great pain. I stand five foot eleven, about 190 pounds. What more do you want to know about me?

FACILITATOR: Well, do you have needs, do you have wants?

SELF: Absolutely. I need proper food, proper exercise, clean air to breathe. I love blue skies and white clouds. I love being by the water. At times I crave beautiful things. I want to be happy and to be fulfilled.

No-self

FACILITATOR: Now I would like your permission to speak to the no-self. Even if you don't understand what this means, would you just allow me please to speak to the no-self, and we'll find out who you are.

NO-SELF: No-self here.

FACILITATOR: Would you tell me about you? Who are you, or better yet, what are you not?

NO-SELF: Well, I'm not the self. I am not the body, not the mind, the thoughts, concepts, sensations, notions, the ideas, opinions, justifications of the self. I'm not the goals, the rationalizations, the beliefs, I'm not the entire belief system of the self. I'm not his flesh, skin, blood, bones, organs, etc.

FACILITATOR: Then what are you?

NO-SELF: I am all things. I am all space and time, all beings, including the self, but not limited to the self. I have no beginning, no end, no birth, no death. I am unborn and undying. Actually, I don't see much difference between me and Big Mind — I am Big Mind, I am the Way. I am the vast empty sky, I am the clouds in that sky, I am the trees, I am the birds, I am all things. I can see the self has his desires, his cravings, his wants, his wishes. The self is limited and restricted to a particular form, body, height and weight. I am unlimited, and unrestricted. I am beyond the self, and yet I embrace the self.

Unique Self
Ordinary Mind is the Way

The self   **No-self**
Ordinary mind   **The Way**

FACILITATOR: I would like now to speak to a third voice. Think of a triangle, like the diagram above, the self being at the left hand side of the triangle, and the no-self being at the right hand side. I now want to talk to that which includes and embraces both the self and the no-self.

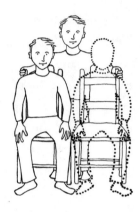

Another way to visualize this that may be helpful is to think of the self and the no-self sitting in two chairs, side by side. I want now to speak to that which is standing behind and above these two chairs, at the apex of the triangle. So you both include and transcend the self and the no-self. I'm going to give you the name the Unique Self. I would like your permission, please, to speak to what I call the Unique Self.

The Unique Self (Beyond self and no-self)

FACILITATOR: OK, who are you?
UNIQUE SELF: I am the Unique Self.
FACILITATOR: Please tell me what it is like to be the Unique Self.
UNIQUE SELF: I notice that as the Unique Self I am absolutely unique. 'Absolutely' is the key word here. There is no one else like me, and I embrace both the self and the no-self.

All of a sudden I have a great appreciation for being who I am. I am the Way, and I am the manifestation of the Way. I am the creator and the creation. I'm absolutely perfect as I am, and yet I need a lot of work. It's a never-ending process of unfolding, and yet I am full of joy and happiness to be who and what I am. There doesn't seem to be any particular conflict, but if there is I embrace it. I am one with my own pain and suffering, and yet I work diligently at alleviating suffering. It's wonderful just to be who I am. I have no need to be anyone or anything else.

I'm not attached to the dualistic view and I'm not attached to the non-dual either. I have the maturity and the wisdom of seeing that I am limited, and limitless. I am not just a particular perspective; I am all perspectives and, at any time, a given perspective. I see that both the dualistic and the non-dual selves are partial, incomplete in and of themselves. Only with the other is each complete.

I see that in the past I, like many other practitioners, have gotten stuck in the absolute, the no-self position, holding that as a preference — no-self over self, the absolute over the relative, not suffering over suffering. But I include both the dual and the nondual. I am an absolutely natural state of mind, a natural state of being. I embrace both not-two and not-one, and I move back and forth freely according to the situation.

I do not seek enlightenment and do not try to get rid of delusion. There's no reason to prefer an enlightened state over a deluded state. Being dual is OK, being non-dual is OK. No preference, that is the Perfect Way — and it is OK for me to have a preference. I prefer chocolate ice cream over vanilla, dark bread over white bread, and I have no preference for or against having preferences.

The self is what we refer to as ordinary mind, or conventional mind. The no-self can also be called the Way. As the Unique

Self, I include ordinary mind and the Way, and that is what we call "ordinary mind is the Way." When Zen people talk about ordinary mind is the Way, this is what they mean: it includes and yet transcends ordinary mind and the Way.

It's like when I'm driving a car. I'm aware of the traffic, I am aware of the cars in front, the cars behind. I'm also able to carry on a conversation with other people in the car. As the Unique Self, I don't get stuck in thinking and being just in the voice of the self, or in the absolute perspective. It's a very natural state of panoramic awareness with the ability to focus on the job at hand. We are all always in this state. This is what is meant by ordinary mind is the Way.

FACILITATOR: Thank you very much for sharing all that. With your permission I would like to move on.

Fear

FACILITATOR: May I now speak to Fear?

FEAR: Fear speaking.

FACILITATOR: Tell me why you are afraid.

FEAR: I have to protect the self. I look out at the world and see everything as not me. So I live in constant anxiety that all the not-me's — and there are infinite not-me's — could harm me or destroy me. They can harm this very body, and also my ideas, my beliefs, my way of putting things together. Everything out there is potentially dangerous, could potentially hurt or even destroy me.

I'm afraid of change, I'm afraid of things not changing. I'm afraid to die, frankly I'm also afraid to live. I'm afraid of suffering and the pain preceding death. I'm afraid of what might happen after death, and I'm afraid that nothing might happen. I'm afraid of being alone, I'm afraid of relationships too. Frankly I'm just afraid.

FACILITATOR: Now I'd like to speak to No-Fear.

No-Fear

NO-FEAR: I'm No-Fear.

FACILITATOR: Why is it that you have no fear — or why is it that you are No-Fear?

NO-FEAR: Because there's no self. When there's no self, when Big Mind is present, there's no reason for fear, because all things are me. It's only when there's a separation between self and others, between subject and object, that there's a threat and there's fear. But as No-Fear there's absolutely no reason for me to be afraid of anything, because nothing can hurt me, nothing can destroy me, nothing can harm me in any way whatsoever, and I can't lose anything, for I am everything.

A lot of the reason fear comes up for the self is that ultimately the self can be lost, can die, can be killed or hurt. It can lose what it owns or what it possesses. I have nothing so I can lose nothing. I am nothing so I can't become anything less. I'm already zero, no-thingness. So absolutely no fear arises. Sickness injury and loss don't affect me or touch me. They're all in the realm of a self, a body, a mind. I am beyond that, I transcend that.

FACILITATOR: Now may I speak to the voice that embraces or includes Fear and No-Fear and goes beyond them both? Let's call it the True Self.

The True Self (Beyond Fear and No-Fear)

TRUE SELF: All right. I'm that voice that transcends Fear and No-Fear.

FACILITATOR: What does that mean?

TRUE SELF: Well, that means that when it's appropriate to be frightened, I'm frightened. It means that I perceive fear as the normal functioning of a human being. It's a warning that there's potential danger, and I should take care and be mindful and aware of the situation.

I also am No-Fear, meaning I have no fear about being afraid. There's no fear about being a human being and having fear or suffering, or making distinctions, or seeing others as not me, even though I always know and come from the place of oneness. It means that I'm very settled in the no-self and yet I function as a mature, wise and compassionate self.

The Dualistic Mind

FACILITATOR: Now I'd like to speak to the Dualistic Mind, please.

DUALISTIC MIND: All right, I'm the Dualistic Mind.

FACILITATOR: Well, why do we call you dualistic? Why do we refer to you as the Dualistic Mind?

DUALISTIC MIND: Because I see things in a way that is dualistic. I mean there's nothing wrong with it, I just see things in terms of right and wrong, good and bad, self and others, me and you. This is just the way it is. This is reality as far as I'm concerned. That tree is not me. It would be deluded to think it is.

So from my standpoint, I am real and I am what's real. I see me, this life, Genpo, as real, and I see things are either right or they're wrong. They're either good or they're bad. There's gray of course, I mean there are some areas of gray. But these kinds of distinctions are essential. Where would we be as a species, as human beings, on all levels, scientifically, morally, ethically, spiritually, economically, where would we be if we weren't able to make distinctions between what's good and bad, right and wrong, this and that, me and you? If I couldn't distinguish myself from you, or my self from my clothing, how would I even know what to do? So, I am reality.

I am truly essential for the survival of the species, and of course I have all kinds of desires. Without desires how would I seek food when I'm hungry? How would I seek shelter when I need it? How would I even seek procreation of the species if I didn't have sexual desires? These are all essential, and it would be ridiculous to think otherwise. In fact it would be so totally nuts and deluded I think it would be a very, very sad person who didn't base their life in me, in dualistic thinking, in Dualistic Mind. You know, I see people who somehow think they're non-dual or they've transcended something, and I mean, they're dangerous. I don't want anything to do with them.

FACILITATOR: Do you think they are deluded?

DUALISTIC MIND: Absolutely. That's what I'm saying. Not only deluded, they're harmful. They're scary. They're scary because if they can't see things dualistically, how do they distinguish between what's right and wrong, what's good and bad, what's healthy and not healthy for themselves and for others, for their children and the world? I think they're a menace.

Frankly I'd almost like to just get rid of them, except that would be wrong. I mean if we could somehow protect ourselves from such people, I think that would be a very intelligent thing to do. They're dangerous. They really are.

Now of course, as I said, I desire to procreate so the species can survive. I need to desire, I need to seek after things, I need to invent and discover. I need to create. I'm a creative force, and if you can't make distinctions, how can you distinguish one color from another, or one shape or form from another? It seems to me that would just be insane. As far as I'm concerned even what is proposed in this book seems like it's bordering on insanity. We have to be able to make distinctions between right and wrong. That's just the way it is.

I don't even want to hear any more about these non-dual reality guys. They make me angry. I'm angry right now about such nonsense — non-dualism, transcendence. I hate people like that. I think they're really a danger, a threat to our world. They have no morals, no ethics. It just seems like they have no boundaries. They don't honor my boundaries. When they speak to you they come too close and their breath stinks, you know, and they're scary, they're really scary. So there you have it.

FACILITATOR: Maybe I'd better speak to the Controller next.

DUALISTIC MIND: All right, I have no problem letting you speak to the Controller, but if you asked to speak to any transcendent voice, I wouldn't let you do that right now. No way, absolutely no way. I don't want anything to do with that.

FACILITATOR: All right. So would you now let me speak to the Controller please?

CONTROLLER: All right. You're speaking with the Controller.

FACILITATOR: So how are you doing?

CONTROLLER: Well, I'm OK. Obviously, that last voice wasn't too happy about the direction you were headed. I had a hard time because he was kind of exposing himself, and just how hateful and angry this whole business is to him. I think he's really threatened, and therefore I need to protect him. I also felt some need to protect the Non-Dual.

FACILITATOR: All right, let me ask you, and I'll understand if you don't want to give me permission, but if you would, please allow me to speak to the Non-Dual Mind.

CONTROLLER: All right I'm a little reluctant, but I'm going to do it. Maybe it will balance something out.

The Non-Dual Mind

FACILITATOR: All right, so you are?

NON-DUAL MIND: I'm the Non-Dual Mind.

FACILITATOR: Please tell me about you.

NON-DUAL MIND: Well, I'm not dual. Obviously I don't see things in a dualistic way. I don't see things as self and others. I don't make that kind of distinction. It's all me. I know that the Dualistic Mind doesn't get that, and sees things in a very fragmented way. But it's all me. Every being and every thing, even the blue sky and the white clouds, the sun, and the ocean, are all me. The birds, they're me. The flowers are me. The insects are me. The mosquitoes are me. I don't make that kind of distinction between self and others. It's not real. Reality is oneness, unity. We're all the same, we're all one. That's reality. This is Absolute Reality.

The Dualistic voice that was speaking a moment ago, he thinks he's real, but he's only the apparent reality, the one that appears to him out of his dualistic mind, that's created by his dualism. In truth, of course it's all me, the Non-Dual Mind. Even the Dualistic is me. So I embrace him, but he certainly does not embrace me. There's no doubt about that. But that's OK, because that's just who he is. I understand that, but he's very limited. His perspective is very limited and therefore very limiting. He'd just as soon get rid of me. Of course he can't. He might be able to get rid of some of those who manifest me. But he can't get rid of me. I'm that which is unborn and therefore I'm undying and untouchable. Before anything is created or comes into existence or into being, that's me. I'm all creations. I'm all things that do come into existence and being.

So I am the unborn and I am also the born. In other words, this very body is the unborn. It appears as the born, but it is the unborn. So this very form is the formless. This very mind is no mind. This very body is no body. This very self is no self. That's just the reality. It's not something we can debate or argue about. It's just the way it is.

Before thinking arises, things are just the way they are. All manifestations are just manifestations of me, the Non-Dual Mind, the unborn, Big Mind. Buddhists call it Buddha Mind. Other religions and cultures have different names for me. Mystics in many spiritual traditions have known about my being, (I don't want to say existence, because I neither exist nor do I not exist, I'm beyond both existing and non-existing), but they've known about me, they've touched me.

So of course, there's no fear in me. Fear doesn't arise in me. There's no desire because I have nothing to desire, there's nothing apart, there's nothing separate. So also there's no seeking in me. Why would I seek anything? I have it all. I am it all. It would be ridiculous to think of seeking. I'm beyond time and space, so where would I go for it? The whole notion of being angry with others, what others are we talking about? Who would be angry, at what or at whom?

I mean there's no me, no self, and no others. So there's no delusion, there's no desire. There's no greed. There's no seeking. There's no aversion, there's no hatred. I'm beyond all that. Those all are manifestations of me, obviously they are me. But I'm not them. I embrace the fear, I embrace the anger, I embrace attachment and all these things, but they do not reach me. They do not touch me. There's no way that they can embrace me. But I embrace them.

FACILITATOR: Thank you. Now I would like now to speak to another voice, the Controller, please.

CONTROLLER: All right. You have my permission, I'm the Controller.

The True Self (Beyond Dual and Non-Dual)

FACILITATOR: I'd like to speak to the voice that both includes and transcends the Dualistic Mind and the Non-Dual Mind. So may I speak to what I call the True Self?

True Self

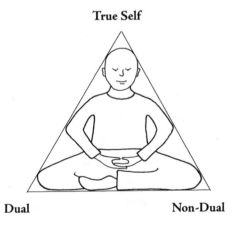

Dual   **Non-Dual**

TRUE SELF: I am the True Self. In other words, I am the one that truly transcends. The Non-Dual is still not truly transcendent because somehow it sees itself as better or greater than the dual, which is still very dualistic.

Usually we call the Dualistic Mind ignorant and deluded because it believes it's separate. The Non-Dual Mind is also deluded in that it is still incomplete, and ignorant because it ignores. It ignores the law of causation, and that's dangerous. It's like burying one's head in the sand. Ignorance is not only a question of not knowing; it is ignoring what's true, what is. In fact not knowing can be a very great wisdom, not knowing is open and without a perspective.

I'm the True Self, the truly transcendent, meaning I really do embrace dualism and non-dualism. I'm totally comfortable, absolutely comfortable, with both, as both, being both. You know the Non-Dual is really fine for sitting on a cushion, but take it to the market and it has a difficult time making the distinction between white and wheat bread, between bagels and donuts. It just has a horrible time there. It has no desires, it has no seeking.

I embrace desires and seeking and fear and distinctions. I embrace them all but I'm not bound by them, I'm not attached to them. I can have a desire, and drop the desire if it's not fulfilled. I can think of, let's say, awakening this entire planet to a greater level of consciousness, and if it doesn't happen in this lifetime, so be it. At least it's worth the effort and the work during this lifetime. I see that the headway made in this lifetime can be carried on by others, because all the others to come are also me, and yet they're not me. I have no problem making the distinction between being dualistic and being non-dual or not-two — and yet, neither two nor one.

I don't get stuck anywhere. I'm completely integrated and

free-functioning, an integrated and free-functioning human being. I move between the dual and non-dual so freely that I'm no longer aware of making the transition. I do it continuously, without any gap or veil between the two. Both are always accessible and available, and the movement is so fast it is indistinguishable. The movement is more than instantaneous. There's just no barrier between these two. I am a little different from the non-dual, because the non-dual is a little bit stuck in being non-dual and preferring it over the dual.

The moment we go to Big Heart, distinctions come back. Witnessing the suffering of other beings, feelings come up, emotions come up, love comes up, passion arises. So great compassion comes out with Big Heart. Coming back into the dual from the non-dual, distinctions arise, and with them compassion. I am Feminine/ Masculine Compassion, but I'm also Big Mind. So I'm more like the yin/yang symbol — Big Mind is the yang aspect, and Big Heart is the yin side, which embraces the yang. If you rotate that symbol, I'm that flow of yin and yang, East and West, North and South. I am that movement of that energy, that flow.

7

The Ten Perfections
of Excellence

Generosity

FACILITATOR: May I speak now to the voice of Generosity?

GENEROSITY: All right, I'm the voice of Generosity.

FACILITATOR: Tell me about yourself.

GENEROSITY: I'm just generous because I find joy in giving. I come from a place of openness and transcendent action, I am all about letting go, surrendering. I am not about holding on, or trying to secure something. There's nothing that brings him more happiness and fulfillment than being generous, giving his life to and for the sake of others. It's kind of like a garden hose. If both the spigot and the nozzle are closed, the water doesn't flow and the garden hose has just got what it's got. If it's got water in it, it's got that much. No more is going in, no more is flowing out. However, if you open both the spigot and the nozzle, it's a never-ending flow. That's like me, Generosity.

The more I give and the more I allow myself to offer, to serve, the more the source continues to flow through me. I become more like a conduit than like a bucket. A bucket you can only fill so much and then it starts overflowing, because it's limited, it's full to its capacity. I think a lot of people go around like buckets. You know, they get filled with so much and then even a little more puts them over the edge, and they can't handle it. With a hose, the flow is never too much. As long as the nozzle is wide open, all the water and pressure that comes in just streams out. So it becomes a continuous flow of that which is beyond the self.

I see that each of us is just a vessel, or you can say a conduit, or a vehicle, for that source, for that energy, for that which is greater than the self, whatever we want to call it. We can call it God, we can call it the Creator, we can call it energy, we can call it Buddha, Dharma — there are so many names we can use for it. But when we allow ourselves to give freely and to be really generous, life is so fulfilling. There's nothing more fulfilling than just being an open conduit, just letting the source flow through.

FACILITATOR: As Generosity, how do you feel when your generosity is not appreciated?

GENEROSITY: The amazing thing is that I cannot dictate what others do with my generosity, I can't have any expectations. If I want the poor, homeless person who is asking me for a few bucks to go buy food with the five or ten dollars I give him, of course I could be disappointed, because he's probably going to buy a bottle of wine. At the same time, I don't need to judge him and I don't need to dictate what he does with my gift.

It's the same with the teaching. I cannot and do not have any expectations or strings attached to what people do with the teachings. Years ago I did. Up to about 1999, I think I really wanted people to use whatever teaching Genpo gave them to further and deepen their practice, to become clearer, to train harder, to sit more, to do better. That was frustrating, it finally ended up with Genpo's burnout in 1994. I don't think he got all the way through that burnout until 1999 with his discovery of the Big Mind process, but even so he found himself attached to his hope and expectation that people really get the process, one hundred percent. It took a few more years before he truly was able to let that go and not care. Since then the process has been far more successful.

Now I just give it away. What people do with it is up to them. It's a gift. They can trash it, they can use it, maybe in another lifetime, maybe this lifetime. They can appreciate it or they can reject it. When he first started doing Big Mind, he wanted people at least to appreciate it. I remember that if there were a hundred people in the room, and maybe five people went away not feeling they really got it, then of course he was disappointed, and they were disappointed. That's pretty good, ninety-five percent, that's not bad, right?

Now I notice close to a hundred percent are getting it, and I think the difference is this not caring. That's what I see. Sometimes he even says it in the beginning of a workshop, "You know, I really don't care whether you get anything out of this or not. I'm just here to have fun with you. I hope you have fun, but if you don't, that's OK. You know, it's a play, enjoy yourself. I think there's nothing more exciting than discovering who you are." They don't have to appreciate it, I give it freely. There are no strings attached. What they want to do with it, that's entirely up to them.

Now I remember one great master, his name was Yamada Roshi. Genpo spent some time with him just before he died, in his eighties. One day Yamada Roshi told him, "You know it wasn't till my seventies that I really got to the place where I didn't care about what people thought of me, or expected of me, or how they saw me. What a liberation! There's nothing like it." But, he said, "until I was seventy or so, I still cared. I still cared how people saw me, what they thought of me, how they appreciated me or didn't. I cared. What a relief when I no longer cared."

That's so important. I call it 'not caring.' I know that sounds kind of negative, however it's really not having any strings attached to what we give or what we offer. Say we give our children money, and they go out and buy candy. All right, that's what they do. If we want them to buy something else, well then give them that, instead of giving them the money, because once you give it away, you've given it away. Let it go, and that will save you so much pain and grief.

FACILITATOR: Is it necessary to get to age seventy or to the point of burnout to realize this?

GENEROSITY: Genpo had to go through a lot of these things the hard way. He's not a quick learner. He learns best intuitively, and by going through things. We all have different ways of learning. There's an old teaching about horses: one kind of horse is really superior, it just catches sight of the whip and it runs. A horse that's not as bright, you have to actually whip, and one who is really thick, you have to whip right to the marrow. That's Genpo. I think he's the kind that had to be beaten to the core.

FACILITATOR: Where were you as Generosity while Genpo was grudging, or having expectations?

GENEROSITY: I was there and it was generosity, but he still had strings attached. I think there can be different kinds of generosity. There can be freely giving, and there can be giving with an expectation, and that expectation could be just to be appreciated. In other words, if it's really freely given, then no one even has to know who gave it. There doesn't have to be any hope of gratitude or appreciation for what you've given. Wanting people to be grateful, or to appreciate, or to return the gift, is not freely giving in the fullest sense of the word. It's somehow giving, but still holding on to the gift, or to what you get back in return.

There's a saying in the Bible about the left hand not knowing what the right hand is doing. We also have a saying in Zen that to give the gift of no fear is the greatest gift. To me, that's the gift of Big Mind, because in Big Mind there's absolutely no fear. It's only when all boundaries have dissolved, or been transcended, that there's no fear, and that is the greatest gift.

That ability to not care, to be detached from expectations, is another gift from Big Mind. I think in our society we're very concerned about how little we care, how selfish and greedy we are, and we realize that we need to care more, we need to have more compassion, we need to have more empathy, we need all that. But what we don't see is the other side of the coin: in some ways we care too much, or we could say we are too attached, and that keeps us from being really free, happy and joyful. If we were free, happy and joyful, everything would flow better, our lives and the whole world.

Can you imagine a world where everybody was free, happy and joyful, where everybody came from a place of generosity and giving freely without any strings attached? Can you just imagine this world? It's almost impossible to imagine, it would be such a different place.

Well, that's our work. That's what we're here to do. That's what this book's about. If enough of us can get to that level of consciousness, I believe the whole planet, would be transformed. I don't know what that percentage is — Ken Wilber says about ten percent. I do believe there is a point, a turning point, and when we reach it worldwide the whole planet will shift its consciousness. That's what we're here to do, and I think we're all in this together. Nobody escapes, we're all in the same boat, we're all on the same planet. It's a global affair. We either make it, or we break it.

There's an old Zen saying, it's a koan, a beautiful koan, one of my favorites. It's about a buffalo that passes through a window, and the koan goes like this: 'A buffalo with its head, horns and four legs all pass through a lattice window. Why is it that its tail gets stuck?'

I think it's one of the most fantastic koans, because it communicates the essence of the whole teaching. In this koan, the head, our conceptual mind, passes through this barrier. The horns, our dualistic mind, also pass through. In other words we reach the non-dual. Now, if the head, four legs and all our ideas and notions are dropped off, why does the tail get stuck, when the tail is so thin and the buffalo so huge? The answer has to do with two things, it always has to do with these two sides of the one reality, the non-dual and the dual, the absolute and the relative.

From the absolute side, of course, what window is there to pass through? From Big Mind there is nothing to pass through and no one to go through it. There's no window, there's no buffalo, there's no self, there's no me, there's no you, there's nothing to pass through, there's no gate. From the absolute, it's gateless.

From the relative side, that tail is all of us on this planet, every sentient being on this planet, and until every sentient being reaches that state we're talking about, where one is free, happy and joyful and truly generous, there's no liberation. We can't go through. That is what they call in Zen the Bodhisattva vow. I vow to liberate all sentient beings, every last sentient being, before I go through myself. It just naturally arises if we clearly see our situation. It's no great mystery. We're all in this together, it's one mind, one body.

FACILITATOR: It sounds like a far cry from not caring.

GENEROSITY: I think it's the counterbalance. The more I don't care, the more I can care, the more I can give. The more detached I am, the more attached to the liberation of all beings I can be.

How could I handle the enormity of the responsibility if I cared too much? You know, I would be limited by my very caring. In other words, when I manifest not caring, I can fully and truly care. So I don't see that as a 'far cry.' I see them as absolutely one.

That's the interplay of Big Mind and Big Heart right there. Big Mind doesn't care. It's completely indifferent. Everything is just as it is, perfect, complete, whole. Big Heart cares about the smallest insect, it simply loves and feels everything, for everyone equally.

FACILITATOR: May I go back and speak to the True Self once again?

TRUE SELF: OK. I'm speaking.

FACILITATOR: I'd like to look at the characteristics of wise or appropriate action. I need some help here. What voice do you suggest I speak to?

Wise or Appropriate Action

TRUE SELF: You can use the triangle again in order to speak to three seemingly distinctively different views of our actions, which Buddhists call the Three Vehicles: the Hinaya, Buddhayana, and Mahayana. These three vehicles, or views, manifest as one free and integrated, unfixed way of living our life.

I'd suggest that you start with the Literal Mind. Then speak to Big Mind. Then you can return to me, as the apex of the triangle: Wise or Appropriate Action.

Literal Mind

FACILITATOR: Then may I speak first to the Literal Mind?

LITERAL MIND: All right. You're speaking to the Literal Mind.

FACILITATOR: Tell me about you.

LITERAL MIND: Well, first of all people sometimes think of me as narrow, or limited, and I don't like those terms as they refer to me. I feel that I take things at face value. I see things in a more straightforward way, a fundamental, orthodox way. I have a valid perspective, in fact I think it's the most honest perspective. If you want to go deep, sometimes you have to dig a narrow hole. You go too broad, you'll have a much harder time getting to the bottom. For example, I know that it is wrong, absolutely wrong, to kill, or to take another life, whether it be a human life or the life of a mosquito. I see that as true, literally true. From my perspective all life is sacred. All life is an extension of my life, and this applies to the life of a whale, or an elephant, or even to the life of an insect. I take this very seriously, that I should not do harm or injure or kill anything. I pay attention to appreciating and supporting all life, from human beings all the way to insects.

I don't steal. I don't take anything that is not given or sold to me, not even so much as a bar of soap. I don't engage in sexual misconduct, or act in a greedy way. I speak what is true, and I do not lie. I do not get intoxicated. I don't speak about others' errors and faults. I neither elevate myself nor blame others. I am not stingy, especially with the Teachings. I do not hate, and I don't allow myself to indulge in anger. I do not speak ill of my teachers, their teachings, and the community.

What is so narrow-minded about me? I follow rules and codes of behavior, and I do my very best not to break them. I believe in the law, both man-made laws, and also the Law of Cause and Effect. I practice doing unto others as I would have them do unto me. I also offer him a lot of confidence and power, and the support of clear boundaries and limits. As far as I'm concerned, this is the way to be both ethical and moral. What is so bad about that?

FACILITATOR: You seem a little defensive. May I speak to another voice, please, if you don't mind?

LITERAL MIND: All right, but I don't think I'm being defensive. I don't feel defensive at all, but you can go ahead.

Big Mind

FACILITATOR: I would like to speak to Big Mind.

BIG MIND: I'm Big Mind.

FACILITATOR: Well how do you see what the Literal Mind was just saying?

BIG MIND: I see things from a different perspective than the Literal Mind. I see that there is nothing that could be hurt or harmed or killed, that it's all a manifestation of Big Mind, of me. There is no one to do the harming or killing or to speak ill of others or to blame, and there is no one to be harmed or killed or to be blamed. There is no subject/object, and for me, even to raise the thought that there is another would be a kind of delusion. There is no other. There's only this, it is all One Mind. There's no separation, no distance between one thing and another. It's all one.

FACILITATOR: All right, well may I speak to a third voice?

BIG MIND: OK.

Wise or Appropriate Action

FACILITATOR: Now I would like to speak to the voice that includes both the Literal and the Big Mind perspective, and transcends them both. So it includes and embraces them, but goes beyond them — the apex of the triangle.

WISE OR APPROPRIATE ACTION: OK, I am that voice.

FACILITATOR: Would you tell me about you?

WISE OR APPROPRIATE ACTION: Well, obviously I embrace the Literal and the Big Mind perspectives. My actions are wise and

Wise or Appropriate Action

Literal Mind   **Big Mind / One Mind**

appropriate. They are in harmony with his position at any given moment, according to time, place and amount. What is appropriate depends on the situation, and changes as the situation changes. His position is always changing. Sometimes he is in the role of teacher, sometimes he is a student. Sometimes he is in the position of being a father, sometimes in the position of being a son. He can find himself in the position of an employee, answering to his board of directors, or as the president dealing with employees working for him. His position is constantly changing with the time, place and situation.

Appropriate action depends also on time. An action that is wise and appropriate at one moment may prove to be inappropriate the next moment. The same is true of place. What is appropriate in one place would not be appropriate in another. The appropriate degree or amount also determines whether an action is wise or not. The duration can either be too much or too little. For example, when he is giving a talk, if he goes on and on and on, even in the right place to the right people, at the right time, it becomes too much. The same is true of an inadequate amount. If he doesn't take, or is not given the right amount of time, his talk becomes inappropriate.

As Wise Action I see that one should not kill, or lie, or steal, or be stingy or greedy, and at the same time I see that everything is empty. There is no one to be harmed and no one to kill, no one to lie or to steal. Those ethical rules come from dualistic thinking, and in my view there is no dualism. I have a non-dual approach. At the same time, I can see the dualistic perspective. I see both the dual and the non-dual and I'm fixated on neither one nor the other. I'm not attached to either one.

So, I do what is most appropriate. In any given situation I respond in the most appropriate and best way. That response comes out of my wisdom, clarity and compassion toward all beings. All life is a manifestation of the One Mind, so I appreciate all life as me. There may be a time when I actually do kill, for example, a mosquito, and yet when I'm sitting outside it would be endless, so I don't even try. If there's one flying above my head in bed at night I might kill it. Generally, of course the most ethical thing would be to do no harm. But there may be an occasion, and it's probably more the exception than the rule, that I would do harm for the greater good, or for the greater cause, the greater reason.

So I might say something seemingly negative about someone or might appear to be greedy or stingy at times, if that were the right thing to do in that moment, the most appropriate thing. I see that everything is relative, that my position or role in a situation, the time, the place, and how much or how little I do, make my response either appropriate or inappropriate. The only guideline for this is my own best judgment, based on the wisdom I have from Big Mind and the compassion coming from a literal understanding of not doing harm, not creating suffering.

I appreciate and respect others' possessions and property. I give freely and generously. I don't act self-centeredly or egotistically. I am truthful unless the circumstances are such that it is more appropriate for me not to be. I am sober, attentive and mindful, and I don't allow myself to get too intoxicated by alcohol, or my own ideas or notions. I refrain from talking about others' errors or faults, and I find ways to be kind and considerate in speech toward others. I don't elevate myself and blame others. I don't put others down in order to build myself up. I am simply generous and nice to others. I do not find fault, and I take full responsibility for action and reaction, for cause and effect. I am generous and giving. I am joyful, friendly and compassionate toward others.

FACILITATOR: Do you ever have doubts about your past actions, and think that after all they may not have been the best course?

WISE OR APPROPRIATE ACTION: Sure. Because what's right or wrong does change according to the situation, according to time and place, and as time moves on what was right one moment may not appear to be right in the future, or what was right in the past may not seem to have been the best decision now, and the best decision now may not be the best decision in the future. It goes back and forth, but I don't know if it does a lot of good to dwell on that. You know, you make the best decision you can as you go along, given the tools you have to work with. I think we have to be as true to that as we can be, and be willing to suffer the consequences, the karmic consequences, when our choices are not the best. But all we can do is work with what we've got.

I think that a lot of religions teach shoulds and should nots, dos and don'ts, out of fear. I have never found that this serves the greater purpose. It's OK in the short term, but in a way it just produces a lot of rigidity and a lot of fear in people. A much more mature way is encouraging each individual to take full responsibility for cause and effect, for action and reaction, for consequences. So the responsibility is thrown back on each individual to make the wisest and most compassionate choices given their own wisdom and compassion. Shoulds and should nots really bind us — 'I should be this, I shouldn't be that, I should do this, I shouldn't do that.' Dropping all that is complete liberation. Wise and appropriate action is who I am

FACILITATOR: No guarantees?

WISE OR APPROPRIATE ACTION: I think there are no guarantees. You have to be willing to take risks and be courageous and just go on. There are no guarantees in life, no insurance that covers our choices.

Perseverance or Right Effort

FACILITATOR: May I speak to another voice?

WISE OR APPROPRIATE ACTION: Yes you may.

FACILITATOR: May I speak to the voice that perseveres?

PERSEVERANCE: I am Perseverance. I persevere. I know that this is an endless process and I also realize that it is easy to get stuck anywhere along the way. Progress can be slow and circle back on itself, but it's more like a spiral, there is progress. So anywhere I am on this circle or spiral is perfect, as long as I don't remain stuck there. I think the beauty of the Big Mind work is that it allows us to learn how to free the mind and unstick from wherever we get stuck.

So my job is to continue to persevere. There is always more

to accomplish, more to aspire to, more to clarify, to deepen, more that we can appreciate and be grateful for. We can always be nicer and kinder, more loving and more compassionate. There's no end to this process, and I'm the one who continues, who keeps going, moves on.

Back in 1971 he was going to call his first book, *To Walk On*. He hasn't written that one yet, but somehow he really liked the title, because right from the beginning he saw that perseverance was what was necessary. To keep going, not to dilly-dally or to remain in any one place too long. But he has gotten stuck — sometimes as long as thirty, thirty-five years in certain places — so he knows it's easy to say and it's hard to do.

In 1997 he saw that he had been stuck since 1971 in the realization that he wanted to liberate all sentient beings, which was what came up for him in that first awakening experience. That's where he got stuck. It wasn't until 1997, while staying on the island of Ameland, in the North Sea off the Netherlands, that he realized, 'I've been stuck here for something like twenty-six years!' When he realized he could drop that as a vow, it felt really liberating.

At that point he thought, 'Well maybe I'm going to stop teaching or I'm going to stop working on this.' But no, it's only deepened and gone further. It stopped being such a burden, because he'd been stuck in this vow, in this decision to give his life to this purpose. So from time to time we see places where we've been stuck for a long, long time. I am the one who perseveres, the voice of Perseverance, who sees these things and just keeps going, keeps going on.

I guess you could say that I am Right Effort — Right Effort meaning that I effort towards effortlessness. I persevere, and yet there is joy in my persevering. I'm not about pushing, I'm not about pulling. I'm about taking one step after another, kind of like the koan, "How do you step off a hundred foot pole?" I'm the one who just takes that next step, whatever that step is. Or if we say we're climbing a ladder, the moment I lift my left foot and put it on to the next rung, my right foot right is stuck. The moment I lift that right foot up and it's unstuck, obviously I'm stuck on the left. Then when I put the left foot up, the right is stuck. It's stick, unstick, stick, unstick — constant movement — and I can't skip any rungs, so I can't leap beyond where I am. I just take the next step, I persevere.

FACILITATOR: It sounds like perseverance has something to do with letting go so you can go further.

PERSEVERANCE: Yes, I guess you could say there's no investment in the results. In other words, you just persevere for the sake of persevering. You simply keep going, and it feels like there's no effort, no trying involved. It's a continuous unfolding, or continuous flowering. It becomes truly effortless. I also have a lot to do with both the Mind that Seeks the Way and the Follower of the Way. There's always further to accomplish, to clarify, to refine.

Opposite of Perseverance

FACILITATOR: Let me speak now to your opposite, the voice of the Opposite of Perseverance. I don't want to give it a name let's just find out who it is. Let me speak to that voice.

OPPOSITE OF PERSEVERANCE: All right, you're speaking to the Opposite of Perseverance.

FACILITATOR: Well, tell me about you.

OPPOSITE OF PERSEVERANCE: I don't see that there's any place to go. Really, there's nothing to do, there's nothing to accomplish. There's no coming or going, no standing still, and no stuckness either. It's absolutely perfect just as it is, everything is just a manifestation of me, or this, or Big Mind. I don't see any need whatsoever to persevere. There's no one to do the going, no one to arrive. There's no problem, and nothing to achieve. There's nothing to attain, no goal, and there's no not achieving the goal.

FACILITATOR: Well, now will you let me speak to the voice that both includes and transcends persevering and this Big Mind perspective?

Transcends Perseverance and the Opposite of Perseverance

TRANSCENDENT: I am the one that includes and yet transcends these two. I embrace the aspiration to continually persevere, and yet I realize that in truth there is no place to go and nothing to do. So I come from a place where everything is perfect and yet there's always further to accomplish. I come from a place where nothing is lacking and yet we can always go deeper and get clearer and do more. I see that there is nothing wrong with where we are, where things are, and they always can improve. They can always get better.

Patience

FACILITATOR: Please let me speak to the voice of Patience.

PATIENCE: I am Patience. First of all, I know that you can't push the river. You can't make the tree grow faster than it's going to grow. You can't make the sun rise quicker than it's going to rise. Things simply happen when they're ready to happen. We very often don't know, actually we never know what will happen. At any given moment our life can change course completely, take a detour, make a complete U-turn, and we don't know one moment before we know.

FACILITATOR: Tell me a little more about yourself.

PATIENCE: I see the bigger picture. I'm aware that transformation takes time. Even though transformation can come suddenly and immediately, it's usually preceded by lots of work. Then a shift will happen, and then there's more work of integrating and stabilizing whatever is achieved or attained. So, I'm just basically very, very patient. I look at things from a larger perspective, and I'm not uptight, I'm not in a hurry. So, I'm patient with others, and I'm also patient with the self.

FACILITATOR: What does that look like?

PATIENCE: I give both the self and others a lot of space, knowing just how difficult life can be and how deeply rooted and strong our habitual patterns are. They're kind of like wagon wheels going through mud over and over again, mud that then dries up and solidifies. Those ruts are really deep and firm. So with negative tendencies, with addictions, with patterns, I take the long view. I don't try to force the plant to grow, I don't try to rush the sunrise, or the sunset either, for that matter.

FACILITATOR: Does patience have to do with letting go?

PATIENCE: Absolutely. As Patience I have to let go of my rush for anything, my impatience towards everything. It doesn't mean that sometimes he doesn't become impatient, but I'm the one who slows him down and reminds him things just simply take time.

I'm the mature voice of Patience. He used to hurry to achieve his goals. He used to be much more anxious about any kind of progress. But over the years I've certainly slowed him down and become much more patient both with him and with others. I'm a kind of holding on as well. I'm holding on to the aspiration to accomplish one's life, to fulfill one's life, to feel that when the day is over, one has managed to accomplish, in a patient way, the things one wants to accomplish in this life.

Zazen (Zen Meditation)

FACILITATOR: May I now speak to the voice of Zen Meditation, or Zazen?

ZAZEN: Yes, you're speaking to the voice of Zazen.

FACILITATOR: So, please tell me about you. Who are you?

ZAZEN: I am the truest, purest and deepest meditation, and I'm really not meditation at all. Meditation is a misnomer. To meditate means to meditate on something, and really a better name for me is "just sitting." I am the purest form of meditation because I do not have an object that I focus on, nor am I seeking anything. I have no goal and no aim. I am the truest because I am pure being, the nothing extra, the I AMness.

When I am present, the self — he — is not present. I am the Non-Seeking Non-Grasping Mind. I am the mind that clings to naught, chases after nothing, and just is. I have no goals, I have no aims, I have no ambitions. I am absolutely and totally satisfied in just being. There is no place to go, nothing to gain, nothing to attain. There's nothing lacking. There's nothing in excess. Everything is absolutely just what it is, which means beyond perfect and imperfect. It is perfect, beyond all dualities of good and bad, right and wrong, beyond all judgments. I am beyond all evaluations. I am beyond all condemnations. I am beyond, I am the state of the transcendent. I am the goal.

When he allows me to be, in other words, when he gets out of the way and stops seeking, allows me to be present, he is absolutely at peace. I am the mind of peace. As they say in the East, I am the mind of nirvana. I am the mind of great liberation. I am that which gives him perfect stillness, perfect equanimity, perfect concentration, even though he is not concentrating. So he is absolutely aware and concentrated. He has panoramic vision as well as acute awareness. This is the state of bliss, of joy, of fulfillment.

I am absolutely indispensable in his life. I am equivalent to the neutral gear in a car. I allow him to move from one gear to another. I am the grease, I am the lubricant.

I am what the self has been seeking and searching for. In a way, I'm also the end of the self. When I am present, there is no self. If he sits long enough, there's much, much less self-clinging. I am the voice that allows his hold on concepts, beliefs and opinions to drop away, so he is not in a state of suffering, alienation, fear or condemnation. Thoughts arise and are let go of because I am non-thinking. I transcend both thinking and not-thinking.

FACILITATOR: You mentioned that you could be called "just sitting." Can you clarify that? Why just sitting instead of just fishing? Or just sleeping?

ZAZEN: I can manifest in any posture — riding on a motorcycle, fishing along the river, running, walking. However, somehow when the spine is erect and the breathing unencumbered by poor posture, I am a deep stillness and a deep state of concentrated energy, even though I'm not about concentrating or making an effort. In fact I'm the complete opposite of effort. There is absolutely no effort necessary for me to be present. Somehow in an erect posture, being quiet and still, I manifest in the purest and most profound way. But I can certainly be present in action.

FACILITATOR: Do you arise spontaneously, or only in certain situations?

ZAZEN: I do arise very naturally when one is in the mountains, or sitting beside a stream or river, or alone in the quietness of the desert. I arise naturally when the environment is conducive. However, one needn't rely on a particular environment; it's important that people learn to be able to be me, or to let go of themselves, in order that I be present, even in the midst of the city, in the midst of the noise and busyness of city life. It's very important that one know how to access me, and I think the easiest way to access me is to shift to the Non-Seeking Non-Grasping Mind or to Big Mind, or to one of the other non-minds like non-thinking, non-striving, and so on.

FACILITATOR: So you're a state that people can access even in the midst of activity, or in the midst of suffering or strife?

ZAZEN: Right, absolutely. Of course that's where training and practice come in. The more one accesses me, the easier and more accessible I am. In the beginning the self fears me. Until the self becomes acquainted with me, there's usually fear of losing one's self. In other words, the mind is busy and active keeping it's self-image alive, maintaining and preserving the very notion of self. I am the moment the bubble pops. I'm the moment where the self is no longer present. Then I am accessible, I'm always here.

FACILITATOR: Is it a loss of self or a suspension of self?

ZAZEN: It can be either, it can be suspension for moments, or it can be a complete loss of self at times. I think the difference between suspension and loss is just the time duration. In that moment, it's eternal. When the self is gone, even for just moments, what is experienced is me, the eternal now, the eternal presence, the eternal present moment. The 'power of now' as Eckhart Tolle put it.

FACILITATOR: What about traditional meditation practices? Anything you want to say?

ZAZEN: A lot of people confuse true meditation with concentration exercises. Now it's true that there are a lot of concentration exercises: concentrating on mantras, or your questions, or focusing on the breath, or counting the breath — these are all valid exercises, and they do lead to me, they can lead to me. In other words, if someone is following their breath in meditation, when they become completely one with breathing, so that there's no one breathing, there's no separate watcher, no separate witness, and there's just breathing, then that's me, I'm there. So that is a way — I don't consider it the best way — but it is a way to get to me, to access me. By counting the breath, they can focus their mind, concentrate it, until they become the count itself or the number itself or the breath itself.

In Zen, there are the puzzles called koans, and people sitting with koans can become me when they become one with the koan. So let's look at one of the koans used in Zen, the koan *Mu*. Traditionally, a student is told to concentrate and become one with Mu. Now, this works, but it usually takes time, sometimes a very long time, even years. At some point, the one doing the concentrating and the object of that concentration merge. If you concentrate or focus on anything long enough, the distinction between subject and object will disappear, and subject and object will come to their true state of oneness. That's the basic true state of being. So the subject/object, or dualistic division will drop away and they'll become Mu.

However, there's a much, much simpler way of solving the koan Mu which can save people years of going in the wrong direction or chasing after something that continually eludes them: the Facilitator (in this case the self) simply asks, "may I speak to the voice of Mu," or "may I speak to Mu?" And then Mu replies, "Yes speaking." All right, now just sit as Mu, and immediately — it's not even immediate, it's instantaneous — at once, it is Mu sitting, it is Mu walking, it is Mu eating, it is Mu drinking a cup of coffee, it is Mu speaking. It is Mu hearing. What's it hearing? Mu. The birds are Mu, the coffee is Mu, the other sounds are all Mu. It's all me. It's all Mu.

People will wrestle with this dichotomy for years and years, and it's just simply — I wouldn't say a waste of time, because there's a lot being learned in this endeavor — but it's not the best use of time. Let's put it that way. The same person could be spending years and years sitting as Mu, sitting as Big Mind, or Great Mind, sitting as the koan, rather than trying to attain it, or trying to grasp it, or trying to realize it.

In another very famous koan a monk comes to a master and asks, "What is Buddha?" and the Master says, "The oak tree in the garden." Well, a student might sit there a long time trying to figure this out, but it can't be solved by reason. Now, is there value in trying to reason it out? Of course, absolutely. They struggle with the dualistic, rational, conceptual, analytical mind long enough and it will come to an end.

However, you can simply ask your self, "May I speak to the oak tree in the garden?" "Yes, I am the oak tree." "So, show me this oak tree." The oak tree stands up, spreads its arms and says, "I am the oak tree." That's it. It's so much simpler and more direct this way than struggling with the intellectual mind that's always asking, "What's he saying? What's the guy asking? How can Buddha be an oak tree or anything else for that matter?" This way seems to short-cut it all, to simply ask, "May I speak to the oak tree in the garden?" and identify as that, and be that. No words are even necessary. I just stand up and spread my arms, I am the oak tree. See!

Transcendent Wisdom

FACILITATOR: Now, may I speak to the voice of Non-Discriminating, or Transcendent Wisdom?
TRANSCENDENT WISDOM: All right, you're speaking to Wisdom.

FACILITATOR: What does this mean, Transcendent Wisdom?

TRANSCENDENT WISDOM: I have abandoned the struggle of ego. I come from a place of trust, complete trust, I am open, compassionate and loving. I don't discriminate, I do not prefer beauty over ugliness, me over you, my ideas over yours. I am about what is, the way things are. I have no preference for this over that, I am not about picking and choosing.

I am also the Wisdom that sees all things as me and that I am all things. Everything that comes into being or existence, and that which is unborn and undying, is all me. I am all form. I am formless. I am emptiness, form is emptiness. Emptiness is form.

Skillful Means

FACILITATOR: May I speak now to the voice of Skillful Means?

SKILLFUL MEANS: I am Skillful Means. My virtue is always to accomplish my goal in the most effective way possible. If I want to get a point across then I will do it in a way that succeeds with the least resistance or conflict.

In the everyday life of the marketplace, Genpo has found that when he acts skillfully, with integrity, he is much more successful. I know how to ask for what I want without setting up resistance or a barrier in others. I don't have to arouse conflict and posturing in others, because that only defeats my purpose. How I ask makes all the difference in the world. I can tell people what I want or wish to have in a way that does not create resentment or hostility. I don't believe in telepathy, that people can read my mind. I know how to ask for what I want without expecting that they will intuit my wishes. I also know how to ask them for what they want without believing that I am going to somehow magically intuit it. Genpo actually learned this years ago in a workshop with a business management expert, Peter Drucker. It has helped him immensely in his life and work.

I am resourceful in using every skill at my disposal, and masterful in employing my wisdom and compassion to bring about realization and awakening. Sometimes I'm referred to as 'expedient means,' and sometimes I'm just downright tricky. I will do what it takes to bring about wisdom, compassion, wakefulness, and awareness. Genpo constantly looks to me in refining his Big Mind process and in all his teaching.

My aim, is always to bring about a state of awareness that takes into consideration that we are all one, and yet we are each absolutely unique in our differences, that true democracy is not thinking that we are all equal and neglecting the fact that we are all different. In other words, my understanding of equality is not that we chop off the legs of someone seven feet tall and add extra inches to someone who is five feet tall to try to make them equal. I appreciate the seven footer as a seven-foot human being, and the five footer as a five-foot human being — absolutely equal, and yet uniquely different.

I appreciate and try to do my best to help people see and appreciate that parent is parent and child is child. Children in their child-ness are absolutely equal to parents in their parent-ness, and I still appreciate their differences. The same is true for teacher and student.

Intention

FACILITATOR: May I speak to the voice of Intention?
INTENTION: Yes, you're speaking to the voice of Intention.

FACILITATOR: Well tell me about you.

INTENTION: I have realized that when Genpo has an intention, or vows to accomplish something, it generally happens that by creating an intention, he is able to continually expand and go beyond his limitations.

His aspirations are to create a transformation of consciousness on this planet, to help all beings to awaken, and to be as clear, compassionate and kind as possible. He aspires to help all those who have not yet realized that we are all one to awaken to the fact that we are all in this together, and that fear, greed, and hatred, which are all based in ignorance, are creating the dire situation that we now face on this planet.

Power

FACILITATOR: May I speak to the voice of Power?

POWER: All right, you're speaking to the voice of Power.

FACILITATOR: Tell me about you.

POWER: I am the power and the ability to manifest the awakened Way that always acts with compassion towards all beings. I know I'm not a voice that is seeking power, because I am power, and we only seek what we are not or what we do not have.

I am the power to manifest in whatever way is necessary in any given situation: to be kind, considerate, loving and embracing; and also to be ruthlessly compassionate, tough love, when necessary. My strength comes from deep realization and awakening, and from the knowledge that all things are empty and without substance, that form is emptiness and emptiness is form, that delusion is enlightenment and enlightenment is delusion, that suffering is nirvana and nirvana is suffering.

As long as I am a human being there is no escape from suffering, and therefore I consciously choose to be a human being and to suffer.

As power I am not about resisting or overcoming situations, but about inhabiting every human emotion and every situation. I realize the wisdom of insecurity. In other words, my power is in realizing that there is no security, there's nothing that we can rely or depend on. Everything is transient, even what appear to be the most solid things are actually in constant flux. We think we can count on something outside our self, or even within, and through deep realization we discover there is no security.

This gives me the freedom to live in the moment, to be present and flexible. I don't get attached to things as easily, nor become dependent on people, ideas, or concepts. This allows me to have concepts and ideas, to love others without an expectation or hope that I am going to be able to possess or control them.

This gives Genpo tremendous power, which if not acknowledged can easily be abused. I feel that people who do not own or acknowledge their own power are more likely to misuse me. There is a saying which is very true, that power corrupts, and absolute power corrupts absolutely.

When I am acknowledged those who own and honor me as a voice within them have a great respect for what I am capable of, that I can manifest both positively and negatively, constructively or destructively. I can be transformative, can transform nations and even the world, or I can destroy, even bring about war and genocide. The less I am owned and respected, the more I will come out in covert ways. It's really important for people in positions of power to truly acknowledge me.

Supreme Wisdom

FACILITATOR: Would you now allow me to speak to the voice of Supreme Wisdom?

SUPREME WISDOM: Voice of Supreme Wisdom speaking.

FACILITATOR: Would you tell me about you?

SUPREME WISDOM: As Supreme Wisdom I both include and transcend ordinary wisdom and Non-Discriminating Wisdom. If we use the diagram of the triangle, I am at the apex; conventional wisdom and Non-Discriminating Wisdom are at the base.

Supreme Wisdom

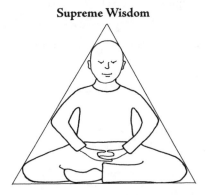

Discriminating Wisdom   Non-Discriminating Wisdom

I am also known as Ultimate Reality, Transcendent Reality, I go beyond both dual and non-dual. I have no preference for one thing over another, and yet I do my best to alleviate suffering when I find suffering and to bring justice when I find injustice.

I am the Wisdom that acts always as compassion in every situation, in every circumstance. My functioning is compassion. I know right from wrong, and I know it's not absolute. It's always relative. It's always dependent on conditions and circumstances.

FACILITATOR: What's your relation to the self?

SUPREME WISDOM: I am both the self and not the self. In other words, I am what could be called the True Self, or beyond self and no-self. I embody Big Mind as well as the individual self. I am the same as the Unique Self, the same as the Integrated Free-Functioning Human Being. I am ordinary mind is the Way, but not in the ordinary sense of the word ordinary. I am both the ordinary and the extraordinary. I am so completely ordinary and simple, it is extraordinary. I am the ordinary mind and the Way, I include both and transcend them.

As the old saying goes, knowledge is power. My understanding is that every aspect of the self, every voice, has its own innate wisdom; that if we would simply allow every voice to be heard, to be appreciated, and to be honored, we as human beings would live a much healthier, happier and joyful life; that by denying or suppressing any aspect we are creating a problem both for the self and for others.

All things, like all children, have a right to be. As in a company, or a firm, the company will thrive and function optimally, with excellence, if every employee knows their job title, job description and function, and who they work for.

I am aware that there is nothing permanent or substantial, that everything is in constant flux, changing all the time. Some of it is perceivable because it happens quickly, and some of it is imperceptible because it happens very slowly, but there is nothing solid and permanent. Everything is interdependent and connected to everything else. No man is an island unto himself.

By appreciating our own mortality and impermanence, we can appreciate each moment of each day more fully and completely. I am conscious and aware of Cause and Effect. In fact, understanding and appreciating Cause and Effect is Zen, or the wisdom of Zen.

I am simple, clear, and logical, but also not necessarily easy to embody or to live. I am very practical, absolutely practical. I am not this, and not that either. I am uncompromising discriminatory wisdom. I am the highest and most profound application of wisdom. I see things as they are, and relate to them from this clear perspective. I go beyond seeing things in a dualistic way, and also in a non-dualistic way. I am the true transcendent. When it is hot, I find some shade, or I take off some clothing. When I am hungry I eat, when I am tired I take a rest or sleep.

8

The Eight Awarenesses of the Awakened Mind

Having Few Desires

FACILITATOR: May I ask you about some other ways you express yourself?

SUPREME WISDOM: Go right ahead.

FACILITATOR: I would like to hear from the one who has few desires.

HAVING FEW DESIRES: Desires are absolutely necessary for the procreation and sustaining of the species. However, along with craving, longing and attachment they also are the cause of dissatisfaction, disappointment and suffering. As the one who both embraces desire and transcends desire, it is important for me to have desires and to know how to be satisfied with what I have and what comes to me.

He doesn't always get what he wants or desires, but I always want what he gets. He does always get what he needs, but not always what he wants. I choose my desires very consciously and make sure that there isn't too much attachment to getting these things. If he becomes too attached to a particular desire or outcome, then he definitely will be disappointed and suffer. It is my job to keep him aware of the consequences of wanting too much. I allow him to want things that I understand may not be possible to have in this lifetime, such as world peace and harmony, but I realize these are ideals or aspirations to work toward that give a sense of purpose and direction for something greater than himself that may not come to realization in this lifetime. He is not attached to the outcome as much as he enjoys the work and effort of moving in this particular direction.

He also has desires that are relatively harmless and easy to fulfill such as the desire for good and sometimes healthy foods that are not going to cause him a problem. I don't allow him to get on any real trip about diet, but he did in his youth and it caused problems for him and others. In the past he has been a strict vegetarian and non-drinker. Now I allow him to eat and drink wisely what he wants but in moderation. He has stopped resisting me on these things but that was not always the case.

He has matured a lot over the years. He now sees that everything that happens is a teaching, even those things he may not have wanted, and that the wise thing to do is learn the lessons as quickly as possible instead of over and over again. Deny or ignore the Law of Causation and the universe will give you feedback. Pay attention to that feedback and the universe will not have to keep giving you more and greater feedback. This is wisdom. Do not think that you are above the Law of Cause and Effect. You will find out no one is.

FACILITATOR: Thank you very much.

Knowing How to Be Satisfied

FACILITATOR: May I ask you about knowing how to be satisfied?

KNOWING HOW TO BE SATISFIED: Yes of course. That is wisdom!

Knowing how to be satisfied with what one has and receives in this life is precisely wisdom. I go hand in hand with having few desires. I am easily satisfied with the things that come my way. I really appreciate life, and all it offers. I don't have a lot of resistance to the way things are.

I am one with cause and effect (karma). I surrender to what is, or you could say acknowledge what is, and then work to improve the situation for the self and others. In fact it is my wish to improve conditions on this planet precisely because I know how to be satisfied with the way things are. Instead of whining and complaining, I truly do something about the world's situation. Most people have it all backwards; it is only by knowing how to be satisfied and feeling empowered and not being a victim that I can accomplish anything truly transformative. As Dr. Phil says, you can't change what you don't acknowledge.

Enjoying Quiet

FACILITATOR: May I please speak to that part of you which enjoys quiet?

ENJOYING QUIET: I enjoy quiet. I really appreciate both being quiet and being in quiet surroundings and environments. I love to sit in meditation and to be around water, on the ocean, near lakes, and rivers. I also love to spend time in the desert and in the mountains. One of my favorite places to hang out is Hawaii, especially Maui.

I don't mind activity either because wherever I am I bring an internal quietness that comes from years of sitting. My mind is silent and still and that allows me to enjoy quietness wherever I am, even in the middle of a busy city like New York, Paris or Tokyo.

This is an aspect of my wisdom too, as well as having few desires and knowing how to be satisfied with what I have. Because my mind is quiet and calm I am really at home wherever I am. I prefer quiet parties, get-togethers, and restaurants, though I am OK if they are not that way, but still my preference is for quiet places over loud and noisy ones.

Diligence

FACILITATOR: Would you now allow me please to speak to that part of you which is diligent?

DILIGENCE: I'm diligent, I'm earnest, I'm persistent, and I apply myself completely, one hundred plus percent to whatever I do. I give my total being, body, mind, and spirit, to every endeavor. I am like a complete bonfire that burns the wood right down to ash. Whatever I do, I do it completely and thoroughly, and I leave no trace behind.

I am a source of joy and fulfillment because I give my whole heart and soul to whatever I am doing. This doesn't mean that I am straining, or even making an effort. I am total, complete commitment. If I give my word or begin a project, I see it through to completion.

I am even diligent about endeavors that I cannot accomplish within this lifetime, such as Genpo's vow to change the consciousness of the world. Sometimes my diligence is like trying to fill a bottomless well with snow, a teaspoonful at a time. Sometimes it is like the little bird who discovers her home in the forest ablaze: flying back and forth, over and over, to the nearby lake, dropping a beakful of water each time to put out the huge forest fire, until she falls, exhausted, into the fire.

Thoughtfulness

FACILITATOR: May I now speak to the one who is thoughtful?

THOUGHTFULNESS: Yes, I am thoughtful and I remember that whatever I do has an effect on everything and everyone else, and that we are all connected, interdependent and interrelated with one another. At the same time we are all absolutely unique and different from one another. Each of us is the whole universe and absolutely perfect just as we are, and at the same time we all are imperfect and have our own faults and shortcomings. The easiest thing to do is criticize and find fault and blame others. In the strictest sense no one is above reproach or beyond criticism.

I remember that everything is empty, insubstantial, and impermanent, and yet, whatever I do matters and has effects on others throughout time and space. When I shift my perspective, I shift my attitude and this transforms me, and everyone around me. When I am negative, when I act from fear and anger, that has a certain effect on people. When I come from a more selfless place, one that is positive and kind, that has a very different effect on others. I remember that it is important to be flexible and not get fixated on things or in a specific perspective. All perspectives have validity and are only partial. No perspective is complete or the Truth, and, I remember that clinging creates suffering, and not to be attached even to non-attachment.

Meditation

FACILITATOR: May I please speak to the voice of Meditation?

MEDITATION: I am the voice of meditation. I can be many things. I can be focus and concentration, I can be equanimity and calmness,

I can be serenity and peace of mind. Sometimes I concentrate on something such as the breath, sometimes on a koan, sometimes I count breaths. I also can be the deepest form of meditation, in which all distinctions between subject and object disappear, and unity with all creation is realized. I offer him the possibility of true rest and peace.

As the highest, most profound form of meditation, I am the mind of non-seeking, non-grasping, and non-thinking. I have no goal or aim when I sit. I am not seeking anything whatsoever, not even in the most subtle way. I embrace both thinking and not-thinking and transcend them.

I allow thoughts to come and go of themselves and I do not chase after any thought, nor do I suppress or deny any thought. Thoughts just come and go freely and I am not disturbed by any of them, they are seen as empty and the arising of wisdom. I do not judge them as either good or bad, right or wrong, this or that. All sounds are the manifestation of Big Mind.

As Big Mind I have no preference for one thing that appears over another. I sit without boundaries or walls and am in total peace and comfort. I do not try to concentrate but am totally concentrated. I am stable and centered without trying or effort. I am Big Mind and there is nothing outside of me or beyond me. I am *the* point but I am completely pointless. As sitting I am the perfect manifestation of just being and non-doing.

Wisdom

FACILITATOR: Please let me speak to the voice of Wisdom.
WISDOM: I am the voice of Wisdom. I am the integration of Tran-

scendent and conventional wisdom. This means I know how to get out of the cold when it's chilly, or to get cool when he's too hot. When I'm hungry I eat, when I'm thirsty I drink, when I'm tired I rest.

I know how to do very basic things that serve him in his life, and I also know that we are all connected and interdependent on one another, and that everything I do has effects on others. Sometimes that effect reaches much farther than can be perceived. I know and understand karma, the Law of Cause and Effect. I know that everything he thinks, speaks, and does has consequences.

I realize that attitude, coming from perspective, has great significance. I try to speak what I know to be the truth, to do what I know to be right, and to think in a way that brings joy and happiness into the world.

I know that my perceptions are always partial and never complete, and therefore I need not get attached to being right. I understand that I cannot judge another without having first walked a mile in his shoes, that everyone — or almost everyone — is doing the best that they can with what they have to work with, that none of us is all good, nor anyone all bad. If we wish to be critical we can criticize anyone, and put a lot of negativity out into the world, and do harm.

In fact all the voices that we have spoken to , and all voices, have their own wisdom. Every voice has both a negative and positive aspect. When we suppress our self, or certain aspects of the self, there are going to be serious, even pathological consequences.

Every aspect and every voice has a right to be heard and acknowledged. There is no true self, and no aspect of self that is not true.

Mindful Speech

FACILITATOR: May I speak now to the voice of Mindful Speech?

MINDFUL SPEECH: Speech can be a very powerful thing both in a positive way and also in a destructive way when used negatively or unconsciously. Through speech we can lift a person's spirit or destroy someone's life. It takes an incredible amount of wisdom, mindfulness, and compassion to not misuse speech.

A person's character can be brought into question very easily and a life destroyed, or even many lives, just by participating in slander or gossip. A person can spend a lifetime building up his or her character and it can be destroyed in a matter of moments through idle slanderous speech. It can happen through self-righteousness or arrogance when someone thinks they are better or more moral than others. If someone is in deep self-denial about themselves and their potential to do the most grievous things then it is easy for them to cast the first stone. It was with great wisdom that Jesus said, "Let him who is without sin cast the first stone."

Sometimes we put others down in order to make ourselves feel better or more important. Sometimes we find fault or blame others in order to evade responsibility for our actions. It is rather easy to find someone's faults if we are looking for them. Somehow it is more difficult to be nice and say kind words to people, and yet we all like to hear nice and kind things about ourselves. Loving and compassionate speech is the hallmark of a mature human being. Being more kind and compassionate toward all beings and speaking lovingly to others is ultimately the path of the human being.

9

Going Forward

As I often say, the Big Mind process is not rocket science. In fact, it's amazingly simple and easy. But the question, "Can I learn from a book?" is bound to arise. The answer is yes, you can. For most people the easiest introduction to the process is to be guided by someone who has mastered it. For those without access to an experienced Facilitator, video and audio recordings (DVDs and CDs) have worked very well. That is why I have provided the recording that accompanies this book.

This book has been designed to make the process accessible to anyone. However, one of the pitfalls, or detours, that comes with reading about Big Mind is that reading naturally involves conceptualizing, and of course the Big Mind process depends on going beyond the conceptual mind. There is, however, a simple antidote that I encourage you to use: meditation.

If you do Big Mind and don't practice sitting, it may be difficult to stabilize and integrate your experiences with the process and really manifest them or embody them in your life. Big Mind is a wonderful tool. But what's true about any practice, any skillful means, is that none of them in and of themselves are enough. So it's good to use other practices as well to deepen your experience.

Just sitting is certainly a skillful means for manifesting and integrating our true nature, or true self, in our life. But we can easily get stuck in this practice and just sit on our stuff. Sure, in the absolute sense it is the most perfect manifestation of our true nature, and we can still stay all screwed up. Some people who've sat for thirty years are difficult to even communicate with because they're so stuck.

So that's not *the* answer either; there really is no answer. The same thing is true with Big Mind. It's a way to help us, but it's not the only answer. So if you combine sitting meditation, Big Mind practice, and everyday practice, you're more likely to manifest your true nature and embody it in your life than if you do just one of those things.

For further integration, I think there needs to be some physical practice too. In the Zen monastery, there was always work to do, a lot of work practice. I think in our day and age, because so much of our work is sedentary, there needs to be some kind of physical movement practice too, whether it be exercising in the gym, running, swimming, skiing, or martial arts, or yoga — I don't say which one you should do, I think you should do what feels fun for you and what you love doing. Find out where your passion is. Some kind of physical activity is vital, because your mind's alertness and awareness is also dependent on the body. If your body is unhealthy and inactive, your mind probably is not going to be really conducive to alert and aware states.

How to Practice

You can practice both sitting meditation and Big Mind at home, on your own, or with friends and family. A good way to practice Big Mind is to go through this book fairly often and ask to speak to the voices included here. Track 3 on the CD accompanying the book is designed to introduce you to the experience of sitting as Non-Seeking Non-Grasping Mind without having to read from the book, which some people might find distracting. You can also practice with the Big Mind DVD's or attend the Big Mind workshops that are presented in locations across America and Europe. The Big Mind website, *www.BigMind.org*, is a good source of information about upcoming workshops and new materials that will help you integrate your practice.

When you learn to work with the Big Mind process, and to facilitate yourself, one of the things that you're doing is learning to shift perspectives, to shift voices, back and forth all the time between the Facilitator and the one being facilitated. That in itself is a fantastic practice, because you're learning to constantly free your mind from a fixed position. That's why I really encourage you to also practice this on your own, not just with a Facilitator.

With a Facilitator you learn because you make those shifts in consciousness effortlessly. On your own, you learn to shift within the shifts. So you're really freeing up your mind. A good Facilitator is one whose mind is so freed up that there is absolutely no hindrance; there is no effort in shifting constantly between being the Facilitator and the states of minds that you're invoking. As a Facilitator you have to be somewhat objective, and yet the voice you're invoking also has to be there completely. Otherwise, everybody you're facilitating is there and you're not, and that doesn't work.

Once you learn to do this for yourself it's amazing what it can do for you, because it means you can be unstuck all the time. After all, the point of all this is to be unstuck all the time. In other words, stick, unstick, stick, unstick: don't stay stuck.

So if we look at progress, or evolution, or we look at accomplishment in our life, the key is to be continually moving on, expanding and growing, clarifying, developing and maturing. The opposite would be getting stuck, staying stuck, so there's no maturing, no developing, no accomplishing, no movement.

What to Do with Your Body while Sitting

As far as I'm concerned, the sitting posture doesn't have to be rigid — in fact I'm against too rigid a posture. When I was trained in the early 1970s at ZCLA the sitting style was a very straight, erect, almost artificial pushing up through the spine that seemed rigid. It's taken me more than thirty years to find a really relaxed and natural posture for myself that doesn't create tension. Sitting is an art, and like any art it takes practice. Rome wasn't built in a day. It takes time.

What we want is to be straight and upright, but it should be more like the posture of a baby. When babies sit, they're very comfortable and relaxed and yet their backs are naturally upright, maintaining the natural curvature of the spine.

If we take the posture either on a cushion or on a chair, we want to make sure that our base is solid. So if we're on a cushion, we want to make sure that both our knees are touching the ground. I personally like the Burmese style the best, which is one foot just in front of the other, not resting on the other leg as in the quarter- or half-lotus, or the full lotus. I've done them all. I sat in the full lotus for more than ten years. I sat half-lotus and quarter-lotus for more than fifteen years. I've sat Burmese for the last twelve years. So I've tried them all, and I think the Burmese style is the least problematic for our knees and our ankles. However, if you don't do it properly, it can create tension in the back, more so than the other sitting postures, so you really want to make sure that you're sitting in a comfortable posture.

If you sit in a chair you want to make sure that both your feet are flat on the ground. If you're short, you might need to place your feet on a cushion or a stool, and if you're tall you might need to place a cushion on your chair. Your knees should be slightly lower than your hips, and your feet firmly on the ground about shoulder-width apart. That creates a pyramid or triangle effect for stability, which is really important.

Another thing that is hard to describe, but so important, is to settle the posture with a swaying motion of your torso and head. When you first take the posture, either on the cushion or in a chair, place your hands on your knees palms up, and sway from side to side. As you move your hips in one direction you sway the body, and then the head in the opposite direction, kind of like a snake, a cobra, moving, making larger then smaller arcs right up the spine, right up the neck, right up to the skull. This is a really wonderful exercise for the spine as well as for your posture. In fact, an M.D. who is an expert on back pain and an acupuncturist, and also was a Tai Chi instructor, told me that this swaying exercise is the best thing you can do for your spine, both when you begin to sit and then the reverse way when you finish the sitting.

Try to do this every time you sit. It really has helped my spine, and loosened up my neck. Sway from the base of the spine, move up the spine through the neck and head. After sitting, reverse the order by starting with the head and moving down the spine, going from small to larger arcs.

Then you want the head and neck to be upright, with your nose in line with your navel. You want your chin slightly lowered but not tucked in. Just slightly lowered, so your chin is not jutting out. Close your mouth with your tongue touching the front palate, and then swallow any air or saliva. That will keep you from salivating, and having to swallow.

As for your eyes — in the traditional Zen way they're lowered at a 45-degree angle, and you just gaze out. That's fine if it works for you, but some people find it very difficult. I think it's fine to close your eyes in a relaxed fashion, and sit that way. The one drawback is that when you first begin sitting meditation you are more likely to get into daydreaming or fantasy if you sit with your eyes closed. So in Zen we say you shouldn't sit with your eyes closed for ten or twenty years. I myself waited twenty years and then I started sitting more with my eyes closed. But I think some people find it much easier to quiet their mind if their eyes are closed.

You should be in an upright position, leaning neither to the left nor right, front nor back. If you compare this to the posture of Rodin's Thinker, it's the complete opposite. It's a non-thinking posture, and since the body and the breath and the mind are one and connected (obviously if they're one they're connected), this posture helps the breath slow down, and the mind slow down. If you are in the right state of mind, in other words if you are in the Non-Seeking Non-Grasping Mind, that will help the breath slow down, and the posture will naturally stay upright. It's just inevitable that the posture itself will start to elongate. If you breathe properly, that will affect the posture in a positive way, and the mind as well. They're all interconnected.

Once you take the posture, take a few deep breaths. Breathe out slowly through the mouth, puckering your lips, then breathe in through the nose slowly, then breathe out again. Do that about three times, then close your mouth and just breathe naturally. After you take several breaths, place your hands in what we call the cosmic, or universal *mudra*, which is the right hand palm-upwards on the lap, the left hand palm-upwards resting on it, with the blades of your hands touching the lower abdomen, resting on your lap, or a couple of inches below the navel. The ends of your thumbs should be lightly touching. You're not pressing them together into a kind of castle, or point. They're just lightly touching each other, so the energies are all connected. Your thumbs should be at about the same level as your navel. You may want to put something on your lap to rest your hands in this position.

What to Do with Your Mind while Sitting

To give you some idea of the most beneficial mind state for meditation let's speak to the Non-Seeking Non-Grasping Mind.

FACILITATOR: Will you allow me to speak to a voice that I think is very helpful in meditation? I am going to give you the name Non-Seeking Non-Grasping Mind. May I speak to the Non-Seeking Non-Grasping Mind at this time please?

NON-SEEKING NON-GRASPING MIND: Yes, you are speaking to the Non-Seeking Non-Grasping Mind.

FACILITATOR: Why do we call you Non-Seeking, Non-Grasping Mind?

NON-SEEKING NON-GRASPING MIND: Because I don't seek after anything and I don't grasp.

FACILITATOR: Why?

NON-SEEKING NON-GRASPING MIND: Because I lack absolutely nothing! For this reason I don't seek, nor do I need to grasp.

FACILITATOR: What I'd like to ask you to do now is just to sit as the Non-Seeking Non-Grasping Mind and just notice what it is like to not be seeking and not be grasping at anything.

NON-SEEKING NON-GRASPING MIND: OK, I will. (Pause)

FACILITATOR: What was that like, sitting as the Non-Seeking Non-Grasping Mind?

NON-SEEKING NON-GRASPING MIND: Amazing, just amazing. I feel no need to seek or to grasp anything. I feel I am totally present, I am the Way, I am Big Mind, I am Big Heart, I am pure being. When I sit like this I have no goal, I have no aim, there is nothing lacking, there is nothing in excess, there is no need to seek anything whatsoever. When I notice seeking starting to arise, I just allow it to come and to go. I don't chase after anything. I don't need to understand, I don't need to comprehend, I don't need to analyze or to judge or to evaluate. I am just sitting. There are no boundaries. I am all things. It's amazing. It's fantastic. I feel totally joyous, and not lacking anything. I could sit like this for a long, long time.

FACILITATOR: Are you hard to find?

NON-SEEKING NON-GRASPING MIND: I think when the self tries to stop seeking, or tries to stop grasping or understanding, he can't do it. Because his very trying, his very effort to do it, to be me, is getting in his way. When he makes the shift and he allows me to be present, in other words when he asks to speak to me, and confirms, "I am the Non-Seeking Non-Grasping Mind," then I am present immediately. It's not a matter of getting to me. It's not in the course of time, nor is it a matter of distance. He's just simply dropping his seeking mind, and identifying with me, the non-seeking mind. Once he's identified as me, once I'm present, there is no effort required. Therefore, he's just here. I give him a complete vacation from all his desiring and seeking and wanting and craving. I am the end of all suffering. I am the mind of peace, the mind of nirvana. I am nirvana.

I am that which the self and all selves are seeking, and I manifest perfectly when he's sitting as me. It's not only a matter of posture. It helps him when he's sitting upright and his spine is not curving forward, but I am not dependent on posture.

FACILITATOR: What if he's afraid of losing you?

NON-SEEKING NON-GRASPING MIND: If he's afraid of losing me, he's going to lose me. In that very fear the self has come in, and he loses me. But he can ask to speak to me once again and I will be here. I am always here.

Sitting meditation is a perfect manifestation of my true nature, or just being. When I just sit as Non-Seeking Non-Grasping Mind I am just being. I'm not in the future, not in the past. This is a state of pure awareness or pure consciousness. When I get up from the sitting posture, whether from a cushion or chair, what's really important is that I then move into what I call Integrated Free-Functioning, a fully aware, very natural state. According to the philosopher Ken Wilber this integrated state of being isn't preconscious as in infancy when we have a kind of pure consciousness, and it isn't how we are when we're in our dualistic voices. It's a post-consciousness awareness. In this state we have all the naturalness and freshness of the vulnerable child, but with all the wisdom and consciousness of mature human beings who act with wisdom and compassion in their daily lives.

All the practices — sitting, Big Mind, and so on — are skillful means, all for the purpose of building character, consciousness, and awareness so that our functioning is truly coming from wisdom and compassion.

This is really the point. It's the point of Zen, it's the point of Buddhism, it's the point of all the great religious and wisdom traditions I know, and it's the point of this book. If more and more of us are not functioning with wisdom and compassion toward all beings — and all beings means all non-living as well as all living beings, in other words, rocks, mountains, the whole earth — if we're not seeing that everything is really oneself or an extension or manifestation of Big Mind, then we fall into fear, jealousy, greed, and hatred, all based on this illusion of separateness. Seeing ourselves as separate and apart from the great earth, from the mountains, rivers and oceans, we tend to abuse one another and the planet itself. So I think it's really critical at this point in time that we wake up and we function with wisdom, compassion and awareness.

Experts tell us that of the seven most lethal potential threats to our survival as a species, and that of almost all living creatures on this planet, two are created by us human beings: global warming and nuclear disaster. If we don't wake up, there might not be a world as we know it in a hundred or so years, maybe even less. We must become really conscious and aware of our effect on this planet and on each other. Only by becoming more conscious and awake will we save ourselves and the planet for our children, grandchildren, great grandchildren, and future generations.

There are many leaders who have realized the urgency of our situation and the necessity of our working together much like rowers on a team harmonizing and synchronizing their efforts for the sake of the whole team. It is now a race not against one another, not that it ever really was, but against our own potential for destroying the very ship we are traveling on.

This is also a time of opportunity, which may prove to be one of the most exciting periods in history. Two of the great forces of the world, the wisdom of the East and the West, are finally merging as one. Obviously, East and West have been coming together for hundreds of years. However, it is really only in the last half century that the Eastern religious traditions have taken root in the West, that the masters of the East have transmitted it to Westerners, and we Westerners have embodied it in a way that is only now truly integrated. The philosophy, religion, psychology, arts and technology that we Westerners live with as part of our heritage are finally merging with the wisdom of the East in the first generation of Western successors in all the various Eastern traditions. Of course, this is a reciprocal process and hopefully the same thing is true in Asia. How else could our world be complete and whole?

My intention in writing this book has been to aid in the effort to raise the level of consciousness on this planet at a time in history when it is so desperately needed. If we as one of many species are going to survive, it is our challenge to help bring about an awakening that up to now was only available to an elite few gifted seekers throughout the various great spiritual traditions. With what we know today technologically and spiritually we have it within our power to solve the greatest of the world's problems, if we are willing to work together with wisdom and compassion, Big Mind and Big Heart.

Genpo Roshi, born Dennis Paul Merzel in Brooklyn NY, grew up in Southern California where he was a champion swimmer and All-American water polo player. He earned a Masters degree from the University of Southern California and was a lifeguard and teacher before being ordained as a Zen monk under Zen Master Taizan Maezumi in 1973. He became Maezumi Roshi's second Dharma Successor in 1980. In 1982 he began teaching throughout Europe and founded the international group he named the Kanzeon (Compassion) Sangha, now centered in Salt Lake City, Utah, with affiliates in France, Poland, Belgium, Germany, England, Malta, and the Netherlands. He received Inka (Zen Master) from Roshi Bernie Glassman in 1996, thereby becoming one of a small group of Westerners recognized as lineage holders in both the Soto and Rinzai Zen traditions. He is also the President of the White Plum Asanga, the worldwide community comprising all the Dharma heirs of Maezumi Roshi, their successors, and the many groups they lead. He lives in Salt Lake City with his wife, Stephanie Young Merzel. His son, Tai Merzel, is an aerospace engineer, and daughter Nicole Merzel is a math major at the University of Puget Sound.